ENCOUNTER WITH CHRIST ON MEDICAL CANCER SURGERY TABLE

EMMANUEL S. OMERE

WESTBOW
PRESS®
A DIVISION OF THOMAS NELSON
& ZONDERVAN

This book is a work of non-fiction. Unless otherwise noted, the author
and the publisher make no explicit guarantees as to the accuracy of
the information contained in this book and in some cases, names of
people and places have been altered to protect their privacy.

WestBow Press books may be ordered through booksellers or by contacting:

WestBow Press
A Division of Thomas Nelson & Zondervan
1663 Liberty Drive
Bloomington, IN 47403
www.westbowpress.com
844-714-3454

Because of the dynamic nature of the Internet, any web addresses or
links contained in this book may have changed since publication and
may no longer be valid. The views expressed in this work are solely those
of the author and do not necessarily reflect the views of the publisher,
and the publisher hereby disclaims any responsibility for them.

Any people depicted in stock imagery provided by Getty Images are
models, and such images are being used for illustrative purposes only.
Certain stock imagery © Getty Images.

Scripture quotations marked KJV are taken from the King James Version.

ISBN: 979-8-3850-2555-8 (sc)
ISBN: 979-8-3850-2556-5 (e)

Library of Congress Control Number: 2024909885

Print information available on the last page.

WestBow Press rev. date: 05/14/2024

DEDICATION

This book is dedicated to the Almighty and everlasting Father, the Lord, the Creator of the ends of the earth, Who fainteth not, neither is He weary and there is no searching of His understanding. He is the One Who giveth power to the faint; and to people like my humble self who have no might or power, He gives us power and He increases our strength so that we can overcome all the physical and spiritual battles from Satan and his evil forces launched against us as well as all challenges of life. May His name be glorified forever in Jesus name

CONTENTS

Chapter 1   Indifference To God's Agenda 1

Chapter 2   Miracle On Cancer Surgical
            Operation Table 11

Chapter 3   Mission Of Arrow Of Cancer
            And Spiritual Ants 33

Chapter 4   Lost In The Wilderness Of Sin 57

Chapter 5   SIN: The Greatest Weapon Of
            Satan (Our Adversary) 88

Chapter 6   God's PlanTo Rescue
            ManFrom Sin 118

Chapter 7   Salvation: The Priceless Gift
            From God 142

Chapter 8   Working Out Your Salvation 172

Chapter 9   The Spiritual Imperatives Of
            Salvation 200

Chapter 10 Are You Ready For His
            Second Coming? 214

ACKNOWLEDGEMENT

I want to acknowledge the support of my wife Mrs. Faith Omere my children and all my friends in Nigeria and in the United States of America, who have been very supportive of my ministry and my call into the service of my creator the Almighty God.

I also want to express my deep appreciation to my senior pastors, Pastor Abiodun David (RO) MFM Boston, Pastor Bamidele Omotosho and Pastor Precious Omolade (RO) MFM Region 109, Ikotun Lagos. Who has been of immense spiritual support to me and my family. Thank you so much.

I also want to express my gratitude to MFM Boston members such as Elder George Obichie (the great encourager), Mama Georgia Okoye, Prof & Mrs Banwo, Wole Ademola just to mention a few.

And to my wonderful brother Imuetinyan Omere, your labor of love cannot be forgotten thank you so much. I also want to thank the Director of Omere International Evangelical & Soul Winning Ministries, Pastor Wilson Adegite.

God bless you all.

PREFACE

Dithering on the salvation of your soul is dangerous. Hesitancy on some issues could be pardoned but not on the matter of the salvation of your soul. It is a matter of necessity deserving of utmost urgent attention because it has to do with where you will spend eternity after death closes your eyes in this world. Indeed, your salvation is very paramount in all matters that concern your life. Whether your soul is saved or not will determine whether you will spend eternity in heaven or hell whenever you die, or when Jesus Christ returns as He has promised. In the book of Romans the Lord, through Apostle Paul, declared thus: **"Wherefore, as by one man sin entered into the world, and death by sin; and so death passed upon all men, for that all have sinned"** (Rom 5:12 KJV). The salvation of your soul and mine is, therefore, necessary because all men and women inherited a sinful nature from Adam and Eve and the consequences of sin are death. There are no exceptions to this divine law. Hear what God said in the Book of 1 Corinthians through Apostle Paul:

> **"Know ye not that the unrighteous shall not inherit the kingdom of God? Be not deceived: neither fornicators, nor idolaters, nor adulterers, nor effeminate, nor abusers of themselves with mankind, Nor thieves, nor covetous, nor drunkards, nor revilers, nor extortioners, shall inherit the kingdom of God"** (1Corinthians 6:9-10)

Nevertheless, God's preoccupation is the salvation of the soul of man from eternal death which became the reward of Adam and Eve following their violation of God's divine law and instructions in regard to the forbidden fruit in the Garden of Eden. Since the wages of Adam's and Eve's sin is death, eternal death for all men and women who are progenies of Adam and Eve (Romans 6:23), God in His Agape love for man unfolded His plan to rescue you and I and the rest of humanity from eternal death through the atoning death of His Son, Jesus Christ Who was the sacrificial Lamb of God.

Dear beloved reader, the salvation of your soul is a process that will be initiated by God. It begins with your acceptance of the finished work on the Cross, the sacrifice for your sins, and that of the whole humanity made by Jesus Christ when He died on the Cross. Your acceptance of Jesus Christ's expiating death will trigger your salvation from your past sins and their penalty (which is eternal death) and the conferment of the right to eternal life on you. It will also give you the power to begin a new life; a life different from your past lifestyle and you will begin to grow daily and become more like your Savior, the Lord Jesus Christ.

I once toyed with the salvation of my soul when I refused to accept God's offer of divine pardon for my sins and snubbed his invitation to His service. But his mercy prevailed and His grace rescued me from the original sin (that of Adam and Eve) and my own personal sins. I met Him on the cancer surgical operation table at Boston Cancer Medical Centre in the United States of America. This book is the story of God's great mercy and grace which rescued me from eternal perdition. Now, I can look forward to receiving eternal life at the return of Jesus Christ. You too must accept this great offer of salvation from your Creator today without further hesitation.

CHAPTER ONE

Indifference To God's Agenda

This boy is born for a special purpose in Benin. He is born to do the work of God, to preach the gospel and be used by God to bring His Light and freedom to several lives and homes in this city and other places in Nigeria and elsewhere in the world, where people are being held in bondage by the power of darkness. Hence, he must be nurtured, trained, and brought up with care in the way of the Lord because of this special reason why he was born".

That was the pronouncements made on the eighth day of my arrival on the planet earth by the servant of God, a pastor of a white garment church in Benin City, Nigeria, who officiated at my naming ceremony many years ago. I was born into a white garment-Christian family and during my Christening ceremony, the prophet emphasized the need for my parents to prepare me for the work for God. According to my mother, the prophet laid emphasis on the fact that I was chosen by God to be His emissary on earth, to preach the gospel of the Lord Jesus Christ not only in Benin City in Nigeria but also elsewhere in the world. Thus right from the day, I arrived on the planet earth, God never left my parents in doubt about His special plan for my life. My mother kept telling me, as I was growing up that *"na work of God you go do".* I grew up to know that the Almighty's agenda for my life is to serve Him in His vineyard as a minister of the gospel. In the Book of Jeremiah chapter Five, we saw a man of God who has a similar destiny. The Lord made this declaration to the Prophet Jeremiah:

> **Before I formed thee in the belly, I knew thee And before thou camest forth out of the womb I sanctified thee And I ordained thee a prophet unto the nations(Jeremiah1:5)**

But while Jeremiah never discountenanced the admonitions of God, in my case they were disregarded not by my parents but by MYSELF. The warning given to my parents during my christening ceremony made my mother to regularly instruct me on good conduct and the fear of God. My mother never left home for either the regular weekly church programs or the Sunday services without me being by her side. She always ensured that she leaves home for the church with me by her side, holding my feeble hand firmly in her motherly and caring hand as we trudge along the rough pathway to the church. Although God have a special interest in me, I never gave Him serious attention early in my life. Not because my parents failed to bring me up in the ways of the Lord but I dislike the idea of working for God. I never wanted to be a pastor in a cassock.

As early as my elementary school days, I didn't like the work of clergy because I felt that being a servant of God will not allow me to achieve what I wanted to achieve in life. In my teenage years, I had no choice but to follow my mother to church and comply with her instructions.This however changed when I became an adult. I began to follow my heart----I love women, I love clubbing, drinking and womanizing and going to fun places to catch fun. I had a maxim then which guided my actions: Only a person that eats one type of soup sticks to one woman". And since I don't eat one type of soup, I eat a variety of soup, then I have to have as many women as possible and enjoy life to the fullest.

Even though I was destined to work for God while growing up and even early in my adult years, I never gave serious thought to it. I used to tell myself that when I get to the US I will work for God. This didn't happen. All through my days at the university, I was not a committed Christian. Yet, it remained in my subconsciousness that I have a call of God upon my life. In my dreams and through an audible voice, God kept prodding me to walk in His way and prepare myself for the reason why I was born- to serve God. In spite of the fact that I still continued to go to church when I became an adult, as my mother had made me do right from my pre-teen and teenage years, I never really had a personal relationship with

Jesus Christ. Nevertheless, the covenant-keeping God kept His plan for my life. He waited patiently for me, waiting for the day that I will yield to His incessant prodding to make me give Him the needed attention.

After schooling, I left Nigeria for the United States and when I got to the US, I continued in my old sinful ways of life. Even though I was a churchgoereven when I got to the US, I was still deep in sinful life. I was still drinking alcohol and engaged in all sorts of fun-seeking activities that will not make God happy. I was a dirty sinner, a chronic womanizer who sees every woman as a sex object. I always went for any beautiful woman who is not married. Indeed they gave me an appellation "anything in a skirt". In the realm of business, I do my business in ungodly ways. Then my goal was to maximize my profits anyhow, in any way I could make the biggest profit as much as possible whether it is godly or not. I didn't care about holiness or righteousness.

I remember a friend of mine, a very close friend with whom I grew up in Benin City, in Edo State, in Nigeria. We went to the same primary school. While I went to the United State after my education in Nigeria, he remained in the country. However, many years after I left Nigeria for the US, I had a reason to be back at home. While at home, I met an old friend who was now working with our family business outfit. I invited him to the US and he too joined us in the States. On getting back to the US, as comrades in sinful ways of life back home in Nigeria, we resumed our old lifestyles again in the US. We were going to clubs together, engaged in drinking alcohol, as well as going out with different women and drinking alcohol. Each time I attended a church service, it was to get a new woman in that church and nothing more.

There was a time I came back to Nigeria along with some white American friends for business purposes. In continuation of my escapades for sinful pleasure, one of my white American friends and I went for Sunday church serviceat a popular Pentecostal church in Lagos, Nigeria, The Redeemed Evangelical Mission (TREM). While ministering during the service, the Church's Senior Pastor, preached against fornication and adultery.

In the course of his ministration, he pointed at his wife who was sitting at the front row and declared:

> "This is my wife since I got married to her, I have never touched another woman. I am contented with her "

I immediately turned to my white American friend who was sitting next to me at the service. My friend asked me:

> "Do you believe this guy?"
> I immediately retorted:
> "Let him say that to the gods and not to
> us because we are here for women"

Each time my friend and I went to the church we usually go home with women. That was the life I was living then in defiance of God's instructions, wishes, and plans for my life.

Located By Uncommon Mercy

In the Book of Romans Chapter 9,Apostle Paul declared thus:

[15] For he saith to Moses, I will have mercy on whom I will have mercy, and I will have compassion on whom I will have compassion.[16] So then it is not of him that willeth, nor of him that runneth, but of God that sheweth mercy.

[17] For the scripture saith unto Pharaoh, Even for this same purpose have I raised thee up, that I might shew my power in thee, and that my name might be declared throughout all the earth. Therefore hath he mercy on whom he will have mercy, and whom he will he hardeneth.

(Romans 9: 15-18 KJV)

Indeed, the merciful God showed me great mercy and compassion. Today, His grace has returned me to His original plan for my life designed for me by Himself while I was still in my mother's womb. By His mercy, I have heeded His divine call to the work of evangelism and soul-winning.

His infinite mercy preserved my life all through the many years of my errant behavior and sinful lifestyle. He made me escape many disasters and tragedies and above all, I am alive and allowed by God to still work for Him in spite of my dirty past. Unfortunately, so many of my friends in the US, with whom I engaged in clubbing, drinking, and womanizing were not that fortunate. Many of them have died in their sins. At least, I can count like four or five of them. But for me, I found favor. No wonder the Bible declared in the Book of Lamentationsthat:

> **It is of the LORD's mercies that we are not consumed, because his compassions fail not. They are new every morning: great is thy faithfulness.**
> **(Lamentations 3:22-23)**

Today I give glory to God because things have changed. I no longer see women as sex objects but consider them to be wonderful creations of God who are meant to serve God's purposes here on earth. I do not see them any longer as sex objects as I used to do when I was in the world. And know the Lord has given me the grace to be committed to His work, especially winning souls into His kingdom and setting the captives of Satan free from their bondage of sin. Praise the Lord.h

CHAPTER TWO

Miracle On Cancer Surgical Operation Table

I never had any premonition during the day that, the night was going to be a night never to be forgotten in my life. Nothing foreboding occurred before I went to bedthat could indicate that something sinister was lurking in my well-lit bedroom, to be unleashed by the devil against me later that night. As usual, I have had a very busy day at work and I couldn't wait for the night to come to have some good rest. Indeed, the night time was usually the time for me to reflect on what happened during the day and also to plan for the following day.So, aftera delicious meal and my night prayers, I went to my bedroom expecting

11

a blissful night rest that my aching body was demanding. Unfortunately, that was not to be.

Soon after I lied on the bed I slept off. Then deep in the night, the enemy came. Satan used a woman to launch a debilitating attack against me. The Satanic missile was fired from home, in Benin City, in Edo State, Nigeria. Prior to that night, I had never been serious with God even though I have been going to the Church. I was never a committed Christian so they could easily get me. I was deep in sinful life. I was drinking alcohol and my hobby was going after women, dating as many as that came my way. I spurned every offer made to me by God to have a change of heart and begin to walk in the path of holiness and righteousness and to return to His plan for my life. I was a recalcitrant child in the hand of a loving and merciful God. This was the situation in which I was when the enemy struck deep in the hours of that night.

The woman came to me in the dream with a cup of coffee and she asked me to drink it. I objected and told her that I don't drink coffee and even if I want to drink coffee, I drink it in the morning, not in the night and now it's too late in the night to drink coffee. She insisted and forced my mouth opened and put the coffee in my mouth. Immediately I began to cough in the dream and the cough became very serious that I coughed out of my sleep. When I woke up I realized it was a Satanic visitation. In the Book of John chapter fourteen, the Lord Jesus Christ declared thus:

> **Hereafter I will not talk much with you for the prince of this world cometh, and hath nothing in me (John 14: 30)**

Yes, Satan came to Jesus Christ but he couldn't found anything incriminating in the Lord. There was no sin in our Lord Jesus Christ's life. However, in my case, dear reader, when the Devil came that night, he found fornication, he found alcohol, he found many sinful things in me and he added to my woes.He gave me CANCER which he packaged as a cup of coffee in the dream. In the morning the cough that started in the dream continued unabated. I then decided to see my primary health physician in Boston, United States.

After examining me, the doctor asked me to do an x-ray, blood test and some other tests. Later he called me at home and told me that he has found some things in the reports of the tests I took and that he needed to refer me to a specialist. At that point in time, the coughing has escalated. So, without hesitation, I went to the specialist he asked me to see at Boston Medical Centre.

The specialist carried out another round of X-rays as well as many other medical examinations on me. At the end of the tests, the specialist told me that I had to undergo a medical surgery. I told him that I do not think that my case, which was a mere cough, requires surgery. I objected to his conclusion. The doctor looked at me straight in the face and declared:

> **"Your case isn't a mere cough! Let me be frank with you, from what I saw on the computer, if you do surgery, you will be alive for three months. If you refuse to do it, you will pass away in your sleep any moment from now".**

The specialist further gave me a scary report that cancer had eaten everything from my head down to my toe. The Doctor's verdict shocked me to my bones marrow–that I had just three months to live! Then a thought quickly ran through my mind:I've just had a baby girl back home in Nigeria whom I have not even seen! Does it mean I will never see this girl and I will just die like that? It then dawned on me that I must go through the operation because I don't want to die yet. So, I called my wife back home in Africa and told her that "hey, I have been told to undergo an operation to deal with the sickness, so begin to pray for me".

Back home in Nigeria, my wife moved into action immediately. She consulted some servants of God who agreed to organize special intercessory prayers for me. And so, a spiritual counter-attack ensued. Forces of the Almighty God arrayed against the forces of darkness who wanted to terminate my life. Here in Boston, in the US, the medical personnel at Boston Cancer Medical Centre, have concluded that my case was purely a medical case and the panacea is a surgical operation whereas back in Africa, my predicament was seen solely as a spiritual attack that requires a spiritual solution.

In the course of preparing the ground for my surgical operation by the doctors, a lot of things happened that I just can't explain. One day, a doctor called me from the hospital and asked me to tell my wife that I have a very critical medical situation. He said I have to explain to her why I needed to go for surgery. Then came the D-Day for my medical operation. Early in the morning of that day, my wife called me from home to give me a report about what is happening on the Spiritual front. She said that during an intense prayer session organized for me, there was a *word of knowledge* that came from the Holy Spirit that my scheduled operation has been canceled. I took her information with a pinch of salt. I said to myself that these people from African have come again with their spiritual superstition. How can a medical operation arranged after thorough medical examinations by top American doctors be dismissed like that, almost with a wave of the hand? I didn't believe her so I went to the hospital for the surgery.

On getting to the hospital, the Boston Cancer Medical Centre, the doctor went to his computer, checked the list of those on appointment for surgery for that day, and discovered that my name was not on the scheduled operations for that day. He announced to me that my surgery has been postponed to give room for more medical tests. At that point I felt no qualm, I agreed with him and went back home. It didn't dawn on me yet that I was in a serious medical problem. I went back home to continue with my normal life. I continue to do them everyday tasks and work I engaged in. And quite oddly, I could not establish any connection between the message from the Holy Spirit that my scheduled medical operation has been canceled in the spiritual realm and the inability of the doctors at Boston Medical Centre to find my name on the list of scheduled operations for my appointed date.

Some days later, the doctor invited me back to the hospital for the third round of serious medical tests. During the series of medical examinations, they put their equipment on my chest; they went to my anus and put their equipment there. I opened my mouth and they thrust something into my throat and it went down to my chest to get what they needed from my chest. They carried out all kinds of examinations on me.

At the end of the examinations that lasted several hours, the reports of the tests scandalized the medical personnel in the hospital. They said from their findings, I was not supposed to be active and walking. I was supposed to be immobile, lying down on a spot unable to move my legs! But here I was not only moving around but also going to work. Then I told the doctor:

"Doc, I am a Christian. I can indeed
be afflicted but I can't be that sick".

The doctor retorted:"I have been the Chief Medical Doctor in this hospital for the past 35 years. I have seen several thousand Christians died in this hospital". I concluded my conversation with the doctor by telling him that if other Christians have been dying in that hospital I will not join them because I am different. He thereafter booked me for another operation appointment. But before I left the hospital, the doctor gave me some advice on the type of foods to eat and those I shouldn't eat the kinds of drink I can drink and the ones to avoid, apparently to aid the proposed surgery. Then I left the hospital.

After stepping out of the hospital, I put a call through to my wife, informing her of the latest developments concerning my health. I told her that the doctor has scheduled me for another surgery appointment. I told her that the doctor insisted that I need to undergo the operation in order that the cough may go. All this while, I didn't disclose to her that the problem was cancer because she had just put to bed and I didn't want to trouble her mind. My wife said there was no problem and the prayer team who had been interceding for me would have to intensify their prayers.

So, back home in Nigeria, the prayer team embarked on another round of powerful prayer sessions that went on for days. The week in which I was supposed to have the operation, my wife called from Nigeria on the first working day of that week, which was Monday, to let me know that during prayers, another **word of knowledge** came out, for the second time, to state that the scheduled operation has again been canceled. I was disturbed by the information from her because I was ready for the operation since the top medical personnel in the Boston Cancer Medical Centre, a hospital reputed globally for their expertise in the treatment of cancer, had carried out several tests on me all of which confirmed I had a serious case of cancer and that surgery is the only solution. I even went beyond the Boston Cancer Medical Centre to confirm that the outcome of their investigations was correct. I visited other specialists in other hospitals whose report was similar to that of the Boston Cancer Medical Centre.

Despite the information from home, I still went to the hospital on the third day of the week I was scheduled to have the operation. It was a Wednesday, the day fixed for the surgery. On getting to the hospital, they checked their computer, as usual, to confirm if my name was on the list of those to be operated upon that day. Alas, my name was missing again! Incidentally, the Chief Medical Doctor whom I have been dealing with was not in town. I learned he traveled. I realized that I had no choice but to go back home. A few weeks later, the Chief Medical Doctor in the hospital called me. He asked me where I was, I told him I was at work. He was shocked to hear that. He didn't believe me. He asked me how I got to work I told him that I drove to work. He said I must be lying, that I couldn't have possibly driven myself to work because of my medical condition which under normal condition should have made me immobile. He asked me to see him unfailingly the following day which I agreed to. I told him that I would see him before I resume work at 2 o'clock.

The following day I went to the hospital to keep the appointment. The doctor carried out a series of examinations on me. He was surprised to see me walking on my legs into his office. He began the examinations by asking me to do a lot of exercises:

1. He asked me to jump up. I jumped up
2. He asked me to stretch my arms. I did
3. He asked me to bend down. I did
4. He asked me to walk briskly. I did.

Emmanuel S. Omere

At the end of the physical examinations, the Cancer Specialist doctor said there was something about my case which he couldn't understand. He said given the condition of my body, I was not supposed to be doing all that I did. He went on to engage me in the following conversation:

"You know what, I don't know who is canceling your name from the Scheduled operation list in the computer.

"How come my name has been missing in your computer?",

I asked him.

"I don't know", he replied.

"I am the only person who has the authority to remove your name from the list and I am not the one responsible for the removal of your name from the schedule. The person that is removing your name wants you to die in your sleep", the doctor declared to me.

He, therefore, booked me for the third time for another operation appointment. Butthis time around, he advised me not to tell anyone so that no one will once again get my name deleted from the computer. I told him that his decision is okay by me. After leaving the hospital, I decided to heed the doctor's advice. I didn't tell my wife the outcome of my meeting with the doctor. Neither did I inform her or anyone else about the fresh surgery appointment. At that time, my first daughter was living with me. Even she was unaware of what happened at my meeting with the doctor.Neither was she aware that I had been scheduled for the third time for an operation.

Encounter With Christ On Cancer Medical Surgery Table

On the day of my third appointment for cancer medical operation, I woke up early and made up my mind to go for the operation no matter what will happen. I called my daughter who was living with me and asked her about her schedule for that day. She said she is heading for school and later in the day she will go to work. I said okay, please just drop me off at the hospital and when you are coming back from work in the evening you will branch at the hospital to take me home. She said okay. And so we took off and headed for the hospital. When I got to the hospital, unlike the two previous occasions, my name was found on the schedule in the computer and so they prepare me for the theatre. As I was being taken into the theatre, I found myself in a battle between Jesus Christ and the Devil.

A voice came to me and declared loud and clear:

> "Yes, at last, you are going in for the operation. You will not come out of the theatre alive." Instantly, strength and courage came from the Lord and I retorted: "I renounce and reject your evil pronouncement in Jesus' name".

I prayed further: "In the powerful name of Jesus Christ, I am going in there and I will come out of the theater alive in Jesus name"

I felt assured by God that all is well and He

is in control. At this point, I didn't remember that spiritual battles have been fought on my behalf back home in Nigeria by the team of pastors that have been praying and interceding for me. It didn't cross my mind at all. Interestingly, as at that time, I wasn't a serious Christian. But my wife back home in Nigeria was a serious Christian. She was engaged in serious spiritual warfare on my behalf. But for me here at Boston, I was just a churchgoer who never had any relationship with Jesus Christ. But yet, His mercy and favor were upon me. At the hour when I desperately needed Him, He came to my rescue.

The Fierce Battles For My Life Surgical Operation Table

As soon as we got into the theatre, I was placed on the operation table so to speak. I saw many doctors in the theatre, all of them in white apparel. As the doctors embarked on the operation, the attack from Satan continued. That evil voice continued to ring in my earsthat I would not come out of the theatre alive. I then realized that

I needed to seek the help of God to be able to come out of the theatre alive and put that evil voice to shame even though I have not been unserious with God. So I began to pray as the doctors were working on me. I began to plead the Blood of Jesus When the doctors saw my lips moving, they were surprised because I wasn't supposed to be conscious as at that time. Butlike the Psalmist, I drew my strength and confidence from the Lord. Right there on the operational table in the theater, I found strength and courage in the powerful name of Jesus Christ.

The Psalmist, King David, had declared thus in Psalm 27, when he was in a similar precarious situation as I was:

> **The Lord is my light and salvation**
> **The Lord is the strength of my life**
> **When the wicked, even my enemies**
> **and myfoes,**
> **Came upon me to eat up my flesh**
> **They stumble and fell**
> **Though an host should encamp**
> **against**

Me, my heart shall not fear
Though war should rise up
against me
In this will I be confident

And so the battles raged on. On the one hand, in the physical realm, the Cancer medical doctors were working to save my live through their knowledge of science and medicine. In the spiritual realm, the Lord Jesus Christ was battling against Satan not only to save my life but also to wrench me out of the Devil's grip to answer His call and fulfill the purposes of God for my life. At this time, the Cancer specialist doctors had already injected with a drug that should knock me out of consciousness. Yet, I was still conscious and alive and saw all they were doing. Their boss asked me "Do you see what we are doing" ? I said yes.

Before I lost consciousness on the operation table, I made a promise to God. I said Lord, I know that the enemy succeeded in afflicting me with this cancer because I refused to do your work. Please give me a second chance. Let me come out of this theatre alive. If I come out of this theatre alive, I will work for just between 5 and 8 months and will begin your work. Later I lost consciousness and they began the operation which lasted for nothing less than seven hours. I later learnt that during the seven-hour operation which was transmitted live to some medical students seated in their classroom via a large screen, the doctors cut my throat region to gain access to my body. What they found in my chest and other inner parts of my body were several hundreds of dead ants. How the ants got there nobody knew except God. So they had to use their equipments to suck out those ants and other foreign things in my body.

I regained consciousness on the same day but not until late in the night. The doctor cameto my bed and asked me if I wanted to sleep in the hospital or go home. I told him I will like to go home so theyreleased me to go home. My daughter took me to the car and drove me home. But leaving the hospital that night was a mistake on my part because when I got home, I went through long hours of excruciating pains. While in this serious pains, I told my that daughter that I was dying and she should call the hospital and let them know that I wasdying. The doctors told her they could not give me any drug yet except paracetamol to relive me of the pain. They had to wait until they get a feedback from the laboratory where they took what they sucked out of my body to.

The Inexplicable Healing

Eventually when the report came out from the laboratory, the doctors were surprised by the outcome. There was nothing serious in the report that could explain how I got the Cancer. Neither did the laboratory tests explained how hundreds of ants walked into my body and what killed them. Indeed, Science cannot explain everything in this world. There are lots of spiritual realities that science and scientists cannot comprehend. Shocked and embarrassed by the reports from the laboratory which defied their expectations for cogent medical and scientific explanations of the cause of the cancer. The doctors agreed that they couldn't found anything serious in me they could attribute the ailment to. They apologized to me for the surgery and stress I had gone through. The surgery was more or less like a medical experiment. Indeed they were apprehensive of a legal action against them by me.

However, I perfectly understood what happened. It was a spiritual healing that took place. That was the result of the weeks and months of fierce battles fought on my behalf by my spiritual intercessors organized for me back home in Nigeria. The healing was the outcome of the spiritual warfare waged by prayer warriors raisedon my behalf. The Lord Jesus Christ demonstrated His mercy and love for me and He answered their prayers.

Indeed my healing had taken place the moment spiritual intercession was commenced by the team of pastors put together by my wife. Each time the word of knowledge came out from their prayer session, announcing the cancellation of the appointment for medical cancer surgery, it was a confirmation of Jesus Christ's victory over Satan who had wanted to use the medical operation to take my life. My healing had taken place in the spiritual realm waiting for only the physical manifestation. That was why I could drive to work and engaged in my other normal activities, in spite of what science and medicine was saying about my so-called cancer –ridden body to the amazement of the Chief Medical Doctor of Boston Cancer Medical Centre. I simply experienced spiritual healing that science could not explain. Indeed, I, a dirty sinner, found uncommon favour in the yes of the Lord. God had preserved my life all through the many years of my sinful life. So many of my friends I know in the US, with whom I engaged in clubbing, drinking and womanizing were not that fortunate. Many of them have died in their sins. At least, I can count like four or five of them.But me, I found favour. No wonder the Bible declared in Romans 9:15-18

15 For he saith to Moses, I will have mercy on whom I will have mercy, and I will have compassion on whom I will have compassion.16 So then it is not of him that willeth, nor of him that runneth, but of God that

sheweth mercy. [17] For the scripture saith unto Pharaoh, Even for this same purpose have I raised thee up, that I might shew my power in thee, and that my name might be declared throughout all the earth. Therefore hath he mercy on whom he will have mercy, andwhom he will he hardeneth. (Romans 9:15-18kjv)

In the words of Prophet Jeremiah, in the Book of Lamentations, it was God's mercies that preserved my life and prevented me from being destroyed by Satan and his evil forces.

CHAPTER THREE

Mission Of Arrow Of Cancer And Spiritual Ants

" **H**ello, good morning
"Good morning sir"

This is Chief Medical doctor, Boston Cancer Medical Centre

"Oh, good morning sir, Mr. Omere on the line"

"Fine, where are you, ?"

"I'm at work"

"Work? That shouldn't be. You mean you are at work? How did you get there?"

"I drove to work"

"Are sure, because what I know about your medical condition wouldn't allow that".

"But that was what happened sir".

"Okay, can you come over tomorrow, I need to see you"

"All right sir, I will be there tomorrow before going to work"

"Thanks very much"

"Bye-bye sir"

The above was the telephone conversation between the Chief Medical Doctor of Boston Cancer Medical Centre, United States, and I. It was part of the preparations for the medical cancer surgery proposed by the hospital as the only cure for my cancer ailment. For the medical personnel in the hospital, the severity of my case requires medical surgery otherwise I would die. Indeed, the cancer medical surgery, for all intent and purposes, was just an attempt to save my life. The top cancer specialist had told me about three weeks before our telephone conversation, that as a matter of fact, I had just three months to live on earth, surgery, or no surgery.

The conclusion of science and medicine about my cancer ailment was that it was a natural disease whose cure can be proffered by scientific medical examination. Although medical investigations can indeed discover nature and cure for diseases and ailments, however, it's been proven, like in my case, that science and medicine do not have explanations and solutions for all diseases and sicknesses. Such was the type of sickness I had. The origin of my ailment was the cup of coffee I was offered in the dream. The coffee in the cup was not ordinary. It was CANCER packaged and branded as a sweet coffee by Satan and the human agent he used in the dream. The enemy planned that immediately I drink the coffee in the dream, what appeared to me as ordinary coffee will turn into spiritual ants as soon as it gets into my body and begin to carry out the evil assignment of eating up all the vital organs in my body. Indeed, immediately I drank the coffee in that dream, the liquid content in the cup was spiritually transformed into several hundred of live ants which began to carry out their deadly mission of destroying my vital organs and within a short time, to terminate my life.

The evidence of the satanic programming of my death came into manifestation even before

I woke up from that dream. Immediately I drank the liquid content in the cup offered to me by the satanic woman in my dream, I began to cough seriously. The cough rapidly graduated into a serious cough so much that I had to cough out of my sleep. At that point, the celebration began in the camp of my enemies. They thought they have gotten me because their plot to afflict me with incurable deadly cancer has worked. In the Book of John the Bible declared thus:

> "The thief cometh not, but for to steal, and to kill, and to destroy; I AM come that they might have life and that they might have it more abundantly." (John 10:10 KJV).

Unknown to the Camp of the enemy, God has His counter-plan against them. Although I was incapable of resisting their attack and thereby escape destruction because of the sinful life I was living then, nevertheless, the Lord used my wife and men of God to stand in the gap for me. My wife assembled men of God, prayer warriors, who picked up the gauntlet and engaged in a fierce spiritual battle against the enemy on my behalf. The Lord that answereth by fire indeed answered them. The Lord destroyed and killed all the spiritual ants the enemy had programmed into my body to eat up the organs of my body. While the doctors at Boston Cancer Medical Centre were seeing death, because according to them, "the Cancer has eaten my body from my head to my toes", the Almighty God was seeing life and perfect health purchased for me by the mercy of God through the intercessory prayers organised for me back home in Nigeria. Indeed, prayer works, I am a living witness to that!!!

The aim of the enemy through the cancer attack was to finish off the evil work they had started in my life since when I was a teenager. The spiritual ants which introduced cancer into my body were meant to prevent me from achieving the purpose of God for my life. Prior to that, the enemy had succeeded in diverting me from the course God set for my life when He created me. God wanted to use me for the work of saving souls on the planet earth. He ordained me from the womb of my mother, according to the prophet who officiated at my naming ceremony, as His instrument to be used in saving people from going to Hell-Fire. Alas, the enemy deceived me to think that purpose was not good enough for me. How can I be a pastor wearing a cassock? How will I then be able to enjoy life? He confused me and make me to decide not to make myself available for the work of God because doing so will not allow me to enjoy life and achieve my personal goals in life.

I fell for the tricks and deceit of the enemy. Rather than being a potent instrument of salvation in the hands of my Creator, I became a weapon of mass destruction in the hand of my enemy-satan.The wayward life that I had live before the cancer sickness came was the handiwork of Satan. The womanizing, the consumption of alcohol, the ungodly ways of doing business, and all sorts of things I did, were all Satan's strategies to confuse, deceive and divert me from fulfilling God's purposes for my life. Satan never wanted me to work for God. However, the salvation of man's soul is very precious to God. And in this end-time era, God is raising many men and women in different parts of the world, who are being used as the end-time army of salvation who God is using to rescue souls from perdition. I was appointed by God to be among this glorious Army.

The work of saving humanity from perdition is very paramount in God's agenda. Evangelism and soul-winning is the heartbeat of God. God is very much in the business of reconciling Himself to humanity even when we human beings have failed to reciprocate His love for us. We have been failing to show love to God from the day Adam and Eve fell in the Garden of Eden. And till today, we are still failing to show love to God. We went out of His purpose for mankind when He created us in the Garden of Eden on the sixth day when He was about to complete His work of creation. Indeed, God has the reason why He created us and His unquantifiable love for Man is demonstrated in His decision to create us in His image. In Genesis chapter 1:26, God explicitly declared this love for mankind when He declared thus:

*'Let us make man in our image,
in our likeness' (Genesis 1:26).*

Thus, God made man in His own image and to further prove His undying love for man, He placed man in the position of authority over all He created on earth. God also prayed for man and blessed him, giving man the power and authority to reproduce, fill the earth and take total control of it as a steward placed in the care of all that He has created.

But lurking around the Garden of Eden with fiendish intent to steal, kill and destroy, just as he did to me through Cancer disease presented to me as coffee in the dream Satan was envious of the power and authority God gave man over all He had created. From the beginning, Satan never wanted man to fulfill God's purposes. He wanted you and I, dear reader, and every other man and woman on earth to fail God. His daily pursuit is to thwart God's plan for humanity, just as he did when he made me stay out of God's plan for my life for about 40 years.

Out of envy, Satan was determined to destroy the human race and usurp the glorious position man occupied. His objective was to eventually rubbish everything God has made which God

Himself had earlier declared as good. God, after a thorough examination of the works of His hands— human beings, the mountains, oceans and big fishes like sharks, whales in it, all kinds of animals, trees, shrubs e.t.c, God made a declaration in just one word to describe what He had done: "**Good**". God was pleased with His work when He created this world. He made everything beautiful and very good as Apostle Paul declared:

> *"For by Him were all things created, that are in Heavens, and that are in earth, visible and invisible, whether they be thrones, or dominions, or principalities, or powers, all things are created by Him and for Him"*, (Colossians 1:16)

While God declared all the works He did all through the six days of His creative works as good, where then did fornication, adultery, alcoholism, fraudulent way of doing businesses, all of which I engaged in before I gave my life to Christ, came from? They all came from Satan. These are his instruments for stealing, killing, and destroying all the good things God has created as Jesus Christ told us in John 10:10. The agenda of Satan to corrupt God's divinely created good works and to annihilate man, the steward that God had put in charge of all He had created, indeed brought corruption to the beautiful and perfect work God had created.The target of Satan's evil plan was man's unique and divine relationship with God. Man was the apple of God's eyes, His beloved creature who has been endowed with authority, power, and control over all the "good things" God has created but Satan was not comfortable with this.

So, Satan confused and deceived Adam and Eve to shun the good plan of God for their lives as he is still doing today to billions of people all over the world. Yes, Lucifer confused and deceived me, someone, who was given the glorious assignment of being a minister of the Gospel of Lord Jesus Christ. The enemy aimed at the relationship God had planned to have with me even before I was born and planned to destroy it. He almost succeeded but for the amazing grace of God.

Indeed, I can say unequivocally, that Satan

hates humanity. He never wanted us to be close to God because he himself has lost the glorious position God gave him before he fell into the sin of pride. His battle against man was, is, and will continue to be to prevent man from enjoying any close relationship with God. His right from the beginning is to displace man from his glorious position of power, authority, and control, which God has given man. This was the position Satan was occupying before he fell. But he lost his power and glory in heaven after he and one-third of Angels in heaven rebelled against God.

Why Satan Envied Man

Long before the creation of the planet earth by God, Satan, along with other Angels, had been created. God, in the Book of Job, when He was conversing with Job over the latter's predicaments, made this fact explicitly clear:

> **"Where were you when I laid the foundation of the earth? Tell Me, if you have understanding. . . when**

the morning stars sang together
and all the sons of God shouted
for joy? (Job 38: 4,7)

The angels were the messengers of Almighty God created by Him purposely for the Angels to do the biddings of God. The Head of these Angels was Lucifer, a specially and beautifully created spiritual being. His name Lucifer, means, the light bearer. He was the most beautiful, the most powerful, and the wisest of all the angels. Lucifer was in charge of praise and worship in Heaven. You can say he was the Choirmaster in heaven.

The Light Bearer

Satan's name, Lucifer, means the Light Bearer or "Day Star." Indeed, Prophet Ezekiel described him as *"the anointed cherub who covers,"* which means he was one of the archangels whose wings covered God's throne in heaven. He is a specially created spirit being, probably the most beautiful, wise, and perfect of God's creations. Let's listen to Prophet Ezekiel's thoughts on Lucifer:

> **Thou hast been in Eden the garden of God; every precious stone [was] thy covering, the sardius, topaz, and the diamond, the beryl, the onyx, and the jasper, the sapphire, the emerald,**
> **and the carbuncle, and gold: the workmanship of thy tabrets and of thy**
> **pipes was prepared in thee in the day that**
> **thou wast created. (Ezekiel 28:13)**

Lucifer (Satan's name before he fell) was a special angel who wielded so much power and influence in heaven. He was the leading Arch Angel and was put in charge of other Angels. But this mighty angel who stood in the radiant glory of God became jealous of his Creator. He became proud and allowed his beauty and power to get into his head and he planned a coup against God. He nursed this plan in his heart:

: "I will ascend into heaven, I will exalt
my throne above the stars of God [angels];
I will also sit [rule] on the mount of the
congregation on the farthest sides of
the north (God's seat of power)
. (Isaiah 14:12-13)

Lucifer became envious of God's authority over the universe, and perhaps for many years, he was nursing the idea of staging a coup against the Almighty God. He planned to mobilize and was indeed busy inducing angels who were under His control to support his rebellion against God. He finally secured the backing of one-third of the angels in heaven against God. And there was commotion and war in heaven:

Then war broke out in heaven. Michael and
his angels fought against the dragon, and

the dragon and his angels fought back.

8 But he was not strong enough, and they

lost their place in heaven. 9 The great

dragon was hurled down—that ancient

serpent called the devil, or Satan, who

leads the whole world astray. He was hurled

to the earth, and his angels with him

Revelation 12:7-9 (NIV)

Satan, The Adversary

From being the Lucifer, The Light Bearer, Lucifer became Satan, the Adversary. He is now the Devil, an arch evil angel who epitomizes everything that is negative and evil. And unfortunately, the evil influence of Satan permeates every sphere of life on the earth which hitherto was perfect before

Satan launched his attack against man and the planet earth. And consequent upon Lucifer's rebellious actions, God had to toss him out of heaven. He fell from grace, power, and authority: Prophet Isaiah celebrated his fall:

> **How you are fallen from heaven, O Lucifer,**
> **son of the morning! How you are cut down**
> **to the ground, you who weakened the nations!**
> **For you have said in your heart: "I will ascend**
> **into heaven, I will exalt my throne above the**
> **stars of God [angels]; I will also sit [rule] on**
> **the mount of the congregation on the farthest**
> **sides of the north [God's seat of power];**
> **. (Isaiah 14:12-15)**

Following Satan's rebellion and its consequences on the works of creation done by God—the heaven and the earth—which have now been polluted by Satan, God had to carry out some cleansing, Satan was sent packing from heaven and banished to the earth. The effect of Satan's banishment to the earth was apparent as the Bible declared in Genesis chapter One:

> **In the beginning, God created the heaven**
> **and the earth. And the earth was without form and void;**
> **and darkness was upon the face of the deep.**Genesis1: 1-2 (KJV)

With the crises in heaven, which was occasioned by Satan's rebellion effectively wiped out, God, continued His works of creation. Firstly, He sent His Spirit to clear away the mess in which the earth was after Satan was banished to earth from heaven. Indeed, Satan had made a negative and polluting impact on the earth Hence the need for the cleansing:

> **And the Spirit of God moved upon the face of the waters. And God said,**
> **Let there be light: and there was light.**
> Genesis1: 2-3 (KJV)

Satan Attacks Mankind

With the creation of Adam, the first man, God can once again invest His authority and power in man whom He so much loved and created in His image.

> **And God blessed them, and God said**
> **unto them, Be fruitful, and multiply, and replenish the earth, and subdue it:**
> **and have dominion over the fish of the**
> **sea, and over the fowl of the air, and over every living thing that moveth upon**

**the earth. And God said, Behold,
I have given you every herb bearing
seed, which is upon the face of
all the
earth, and every tree, in the which
is the
fruit of a tree yielding seed; to
you it
shall be for meat. And to every
beast
of the earth, and to every fowl of
the air,
and to every thing that creepeth
upon
the earth, wherein there is life, I
have
given every green herb for meat:
and it was so**
Genesis1: 28-31

Upon his arrival on planet earth, Satan met Adam, the first man, in the position of God-appointed Steward with power and authority over all God has created. Man was even made to be a little lower than the angels:

> **For thou hast made him a little lower than the angels, and hast crowned him with glory and honour.**
> Psalm 8:5

Satan could not tolerate man, who, he believed is now in control of authority, power, and influence that he had lost in heaven due to his own rebellion against God. Satan and his demons were not ready to concede in their fight against God. He opened another chapter in his eternal battle against God this time, the prime target was Man and the venue of the battle was the Garden of Eden, from where man was to wield his God-given authority and power over all things that God had created. Satan coveted this power and authority wielded by man and he launched attacks against man in the Garden of Eden.

Attack On Man And The Grand Deception

To dethrone man from his position of authority and power over all that God has created, Satan knew that he would need to introduce SIN. Sin is the only thing that can make God turn against His beloved creature—MAN. God hates sin and He wouldn't tolerate it. Satan knew this quite all right so, he perfected a plan to make man disobey God. He would need to deceive Adam and Eve into doing exactly what God asked them not to do. And doing contrary to God's instructions amounts to serious sin with dire consequences for man's continued divine relationship with God.

Using his devilish power of deception and craftiness, Satan convinced the first man and his wife to disregard the instruction and commandments of God. They bought the lie that Satan sold to them with the following attendant consequences:

a. Sin entered into the world through Adam and Eve's disobedience.

b. Adam and Eve's disobedience which came via Satan's trickery and luring of the first man and woman into sin also brought in its wake spiritual DEATH

c. Man was spiritually disconnected from God, his Source

d. Man cut himself off from the guidance, direction, and blessings of God.

e. Physical death became inevitable.

The subsequent history of humankind has been a struggle against Satan the deadly and eternal enemy. Satan became the enemy of God as well as the enemy of man. Little wonder, Apostle Paul declared in Ephesians 6:13:

> **"For we wrestle not against flesh and blood,**
> **but against principalities, against wickedness**
> **in high places".**

Satan has not stopped his evil machinations against man. He has continued to be the Great Adversary to God and Man. Today, everyone can see that the works of creation which God declared as good are no longer good and beautiful anymore. They have been polluted by Satan. Hitherto, there were no pains, sickness, and death because they were not in the original creations. However, the sins of pride, envy, gluttony, lust, anger, greed, and sloth which are all consequences of Satan diabolical acts and man's fall to the tricks and deception of Satan, brought pollution and perversion to the hitherto perfect and good works of God.

Time To Reject Satan's Deception

Dear reader, I want you to know that Satan has not stopped deceiving people. He deceived and lured me into rejecting God's good plan for my life until God showed His mercy to me and wrenched me from his evil grip of womanizing, alcohol, and sorts of pleasure of the flesh. In fact in this end-time, Satan, the enemy of our soul has upped his game. He is employing all kinds of tricks to lure people into sinning against God and sending them to Hell-Fire. Would you allow yourself to be deceived again by Satan? Won't you rather accept the works on the Cross of Calvary which were meant to redeem your soul from the deception of Satan and ultimate destruction? The ball is in your court. God is waiting for you to take that decision and get your freedom back as I got mine back, right on the Cancer medical surgery table at Boston Cancer Medical Centre in the United States of America. Amen. Jesus Christ is waiting for you to accept His offer of Salvation—the finished work on the Cross of Calvary:

> **Here I am! I stand at the door and knock. If anyone hears my voice and**
> **opens the door, I will come in and eat with that person, and they with me.**
> **Revelation 3:20**

God bless you as you take that decision today. Amen.

CHAPTER FOUR

Lost In The Wilderness Of Sin

Amazing Grace, how sweet the sound
That saved a wretch like me
I once was lost, but now am found
Was blind but now I see

Was Grace that taught my heart to fear
And Grace, my fears relieved
How precious did that Grace appear
The hour I first believed

The Caribbean Cultural Centre in Boston, Massachusetts, in the United States of America, was established to be a place for the promotion of the cultures and the arts of the Caribbean people. It is a placemeant for the celebration and showcasing of theCaribbean artistic, musical, literary, culinary, political and social elements that are part of the everyday life of the Caribbean people all over the world. It was a place where you will find people from all races and different countries and continentsfraternizing in a relaxed atmosphere. The Club was alsorendezvous for fun seekers, looking for all kinds of sensual pleasures that night clubs offer to their patrons.

In my days in the wilderness of sin, this particular Caribbean Cultural center served as the place I usually go to gratify my appetites for women, alcohol, and food. Night clubs serve as rendezvous of fun for fun-seekers who hide under the cover of the night to also perpetrate all kinds of things not approved by God. In a way, these night clubs are Satan's slaughtering slabs where so many lives and destinies have been prematurely terminated. In the wilderness of sin, anything goes. Any act or behavior is deemed fit and proper as long as your desires are met.

On many nights, I have visited this particular night clubs in the company of my friends. In those days when we were firmly in the grip of Satan, the night clubs are a place we do go to after hard work during the day. We usually have plenty to eat and drink. And believe you me, there was never a time we visited that we didn't go home with ladies. The ladies were never in short supply; they were always available in different colors and shapes. All you need to do is to just pick your choice and you are on your way home for a fun-filled night!!!

In those days, Satan used this club and others which I frequented in the company of my friends to hold me down in the wilderness of sin. I was immersed in a dirty and sinful lifestyle. In the Book of Roman Chapter one, Apostle Paul gave a vivid description of the heart of nightcrawlers who indulge in nightclubbing:

> **Claiming to be wise, they became fools(professing to be smart, they made simpletonsof themselves... therefore God gave them up in the lusts of their (own hearts to**

> **sexual impurity, to dishonoring their bodies among themselves abandoning them to the power of sin (Romans 1:22-24)**

In verse 28, Apostle Paul summed up the irrational thinking of those who are lost in the wilderness of sin just as I was many years ago:

> **And so, since they did not see fit to acknowledge God or approve of Him, or consider Him worth the knowing God gave them over to a baseand condemned mind to do things not proper or decentbut loathsome**
> **(Romans 1:22-24 AMP)**

Again, in the Book of First Timothy, Chapter 5, Apostle Paul, in the course of advising Timothy on how to manage the affairs of married women and widows in the church warned against indulgence in worldly pleasures. The man of God declared thus to Timothy that:

Whereas she who lives in pleasure and self-gratification(giving herself up to luxury and self-indulgence) is dead while she (sill) lives (1Timothy5:6 AMP)

My beloved reader, it is pertinent to know that this warning is not only applicable to all women but to all men also. Indulgence in worldly pleasures usually leads to spiritual separation from God. It ultimately leads to spiritual death as well as eternal death and separation from God in hellfire. In First John Chapter 2, Apostle John, just as Apostle Paul did, also gave Christians serious warning against night clubbing, womanizing, alcoholism, and all other sinful pleasures which our flesh always asks for. Listen to Apostle John:

Do not love the world or the things in the world.
If anyone loves the world, the love of the Father

is not in him. For all that is in the world—the desires of the flesh and the desires of the eyes and the pride of life—is not from the Father but is from the world. And the world is passing away along with its desires, but whoever does the will of God abides forever (1John 2:15-17)

Beloved reader, I did not only loved the world, but I was also deeply immersed in sinful pleasures of the world. These sinful pleasures are the magnetic force that Satan is using to pull all-night crawlers who patronize night clubs wherever they are on the face of the earth, into his bondages. The sinful pleasures are the free train rides that are taking several millions of people into HELL-FIRE. Unfortunately, these sinful pleasures were my pastimewhen I was in the wilderness of sin. Sexual immorality, gluttony, greedy desires to be rich by conducting my business in any way it can fetch me good profits whether it is Godly or not as well as the pride of life—believing in my achievements characterized my lifestyle in my years in the wilderness of sin. But thanks be to the loving Father, the Father of all mercies, using the word of Apostle Paul. He never gave up on me and His mercy redeemed me from perdition.

One Saturday night, not too long after my Cancer operation, I experienced deliverance from the alluring influence and power of the satanic spirit behind night clubbing and the wilderness of sin. That night, I had just dropped of a client and I drove past the street where that night club—the Caribbean Cultural Centre—which I used to patronize before I gave my life to Christ was. As I was approaching the Club, a thought which I didn't immediately know was from Satan, came to my mind. I felt a strong urge in my mind to just branch at the club and see what was going on in there. I didn't know immediately that it was Satan's attempt to drag me back to my vomit. As I was getting close to the Club, I prayed a useless prayer:

"God, if there is a free parking slot in this club's parking space, that means you want me to visit the place tonight.

But If I do not see any vacant parking
slot, then you do not want me to go
there."

Unfortunately for me, and because Satan was
hell-bent in drawing me back into a sinful life,
just as I was about to get to the place, I saw two
carspulling out of the club's Car Park, thereby
creating two parking slots for me instead of the one
I had asked for. But again, that night, the mercy
of God saved me from going back to my vomit.
Indeed, His mercies upon my life are enduring
and I will always thank God for that. Just as I was
about entering the Club's car park, I began to ask
myself some questions:

"Hey, what if I got into this club and
one drunk
guy just shoot me What will happen
to me?
Isn't that untimely death?

Immediately God woke me up from my spiritual
slumber. I started asking for forgiveness from God
and I drove away.

Sin Kills

Apostle Paul in his treatise to early Christians living in Ephesus made them to know the devastating effects of sin on their relationship with God. Sin kills and indeed, it Killed Adam and Eve in the Garden of Eden. Sin was and still remains the potent weapon in the hand of Satan in achieving his diabolical plot against man. One of the dire consequences of Adam's and Eve's sins in the Garden of Eden was that the moment they disobeyed God, they became dead spiritually.

> **And you hath he quickened, who were**
> **dead in trespasses and sins;**
> **Wherein in**
> **time past ye walked according to the course**
> **of this world, according to the prince of the**
> **power of the air, the spirit that now worketh**
> **in the children of disobedience: Among whom**

also we all had our conversation in times past
in the lusts of our flesh, fulfilling the desires of
the flesh and of the mind; and were by nature
the children of wrath, even as others. But God,
who is rich in mercy, for his great love wherewith
he loved us, Even when we were dead in sins, hath
quickened us together with Christ, (by grace ye
are saved;) And hath raised us up together, and
made us sit together in heavenly places in Christ Jesus:
Ephesians 2:1-6 (KJV)

As many people that still remain in sin, who refuse to accept God's free remedy against sin, which is salvation through Jesus Christ, will remain in their spiritual death and separation from God who forever is the source of life, blessings, wealth, power, glory, peace and every other thing that man needs to live a meaningful life here on earth. It is therefore dangerous to follow the ways of the spirit of disobedience, that is, Satan. Satan's ways are the attitude, belief, culture, and traditions and the philosophy of this world.

Sin Killed The Plan Of God For Adam And Eve

There is no gainsaying the fact that Satan succeeded in his evil plot against mankind when he lured the first man and the first woman into acting contrary to the instructions God gave them, thereby making them to sin against God. Today, Satan is still ever busy, doing this same thing. He is daily pre-occupied with one main objective— luring billions of people on the planet earth into sin thereby preventing them from having a relationship with their Creator. Dear reader, will you allow him to ensnare you into sin?

The consequences of Adam's and Eve's disobedience to God's commandments were grievous. Their failure to adhere strictly to God's instructions brought in its wake eternal spiritual disconnection and separation from God.

Owing to their sins of disobedience, Adam and Eve not only lost their place in the Garden of Eden but also their unique relationship with God.

Their punishment, which was eternal banishment from the presence of God and severance of relationship with their creator, was transmitted to their progenies and consequently, you and I, and the rest of humanity were separated or disconnected from God Who is the Source of both physical and spiritual lives.

The import of this separation from God is such that if a person dies physically here on earth without being first reconnected to God through the atoning blood of Jesus Christ, that was shed on the cross of Calvary for the remission of sins, such a person will forever be separated from God. His or her eternal home will be where God's enemies live---HELL-FIRE, the place God created for Satan and other fallen Angels.

That is how serious the consequences of Adam's and Eve's sins were. Indeed, up till today,

God cannot tolerate sins because He is a holy God. Our sins are still separating us from God as Prophet Isaiah declared:

Behold, the Lord's hand is not shortened,
that it cannot save; neither his ear heavy,
that it cannot hear: But your iniquities have
separated between you and your God, and your
sins have hid his face from you,
that he will not hear. For your hands are
defiled with blood, and your fingers with
iniquity; your lips have spoken lies, your
tongue hath muttered perverseness.
(Isaiah 59:1-3)

In Psalm 22:1, we saw the lamentations of David regarding the impact of his sins on his relationship with God. God had turned His eyes

69

away from David because of sins and he had to cry out:

> My <u>God</u>, my God, why Have you forsaken me?"
> (<u>Psalm 22:1</u>).

Even our Lord Jesus Christ, while on the cross of Calvary, bearing the burden of the sins of the whole world, God had to look the other way because He discountenanced sins which he was bearing at that moment.

> **"And about the ninth hour [mid-afternoon]**
> **Jesus cried out with a loud voice, saying,**
> **'Eli, Eli, lama sabachthani?' that is,**
> **'My God,**
> **My God, why have You forsaken Me?"**
> (<u>Matthew 27:46</u>; see also <u>Mark 15:34</u>).

Indeed, what can make God to abandon His beloved Son in Whom He is well pleased must be a serious matter. And that matter was the SIN of the whole world. However, thanks be to God who through Jesus Christ His Son, offered to reconcile us to Himself if only we can accept the **FINISHED WORK** on the cross. This is the grace of God. Through His grace, forgiveness, and mercy, God is reconnecting us to Himself. He is restoring us through the precious Blood of Jesus Christ that was shed on the Cross. He is redeeming us and re-establishing the relationship that was broken by sin in the Garden of Eden.

Sin Nurtures Cravings And Desires Of The Flesh

Apostle Paul talked about the cravings and desires of the flesh in his letter to the Ephesians. He noted that before the Christians in Ephesus met the Lord, they were following the hankering and yearnings of their sinful flesh. Dear reader, all of us were once like that. We were all living our lives like the early Christians in Ephesus that Apostle Paul preached to in his treatise. Indeed anyone who is not redeemed by the atoning blood of the Lamb of God is bound to pander to the desires of his or her flesh. That is natural. No wonder Apostle Paul canvassed the reining of the flesh and subjecting it to the control of the Holy Spirit.

The question I want to ask you, at this juncture, dear reader, is: "are you putting your flesh under check?" Do you know that your flesh must die before you can be alive again in the spirit? Yes, indeed our flesh must die. Let us listen to Apostle Paul again:

> **For if ye live after the flesh, ye shall die: but if ye, through the Spirit, do mortify the deeds of the body, ye shall live**.
> Romans 8:13 (KJV)

Man's spiritual death and separation from God was the ultimate objective of Satan's attack on mankind in the Garden of Eden. He succeeded in luring Adam and Eve into sinning against God and they were consequently separated and cut off from God. They died spiritual death which God had earlier on warned them against.

But of the tree of the knowledge of good and evil, thou shalt not eat of it:
for in the day that thou eatest thereof
thou shalt surely die
(Genesis 2:17) (KJV)

What followed their disobedience was spiritual death. There was no more connection with their creator. Immediately Adam and Eve transgressed against God's divine law, their nature became evil. They no longer saw anything wrong in following dictates of their evil nature and above all, they could tolerate and listen to Satan.

Sadly, there was, and there is up till today, no enmity between the sinful nature of man and Satan, the originator of sin. The hitherto divine and spiritual nature of man was gone. Thus they are now being controlled by their depraved instinct. Henceforth, it is the dictates of their human reasoning that guide their thoughts and actions; it is no longer the Spirit of God.:

73

**8 And they heard the sound of the Lord
God walking in the garden in the cool
of the day, and the man and his wife hid
themselves from the presence of the
Lord God among the trees of the garden.**
Genesis 3:8(KJV)

Adam and Eve had to hide from God. They ran away from God's presence, they hide from His caring and affectionate presence. Hitherto, they had lived in perfect accord and peace with God. They had no cause to be scared of Him or be ashamed to be in His presence. Indeed, as the stewards of the Garden of Eden and the whole earth, who had been given dominion and authority over all that God created, they were always free to interact with God and have a nice time with Him in the cool of the evening. But after sinning against God, after the fall, they lost every right and privilege to come boldly into the presence of God. They lost their spiritual connection to God, their rights, privileges as God's beloved as well as their right to dominate all God had created. They also lost their home—the Garden of Eden, as they were driven out of it. This is still happening today. God cannot tolerate any connection or relationship with you as long as you dwell in sins. You need to do away with sins and embrace His gift of salvation being offered through the Lord Jesus Christ.

The Bible declared that Adam and Eve lost the divine aura which had enveloped them like a garment that covered their nakedness. That was the divine glory of God that covered them. Without it we will be naked physically and spiritually:

> **And the eyes of them both were opened,**
> **and they knew that they were naked; and**
> **they sewed fig leaves together, and made themselves aprons.**
> Genesis 3:7(KJV)

The problem of humanity has been contending with since the fall of our first parents is the flagrant disobedience of God's commandment and instructions. Oftentimes, we do not care about the warnings of God and the dire consequences of failing to heed the warnings. Unfortunately, we often ignore the pleadings of the Spirit of God who speaks to us through our consciences and we rather choose to indulge in sinful things that make God unhappy. It is alarming how people think they can get away with the consequences of their sins just as Adam and Eve had thought. They always forget that God is all-knowing; God is everywhere watching our actions. In the words of the Psalmist, people who are disobedient to God often say in their hearts:

> **He hath said in his heart, God hath forgotten: he hideth his face; he will**
> **never see it**
> (Psalm 10:11)

But is it possible to fool God whose eyes rove around the world? Can anyone be so foolish to think that his or her acts of lying, fornication, stealing, adultery, backbiting, murder, e.t.c. will escape the roving eyes of the Lord? No, I do not think so:

> **For the eyes of the LORD run to and fro**
> **throughout the whole earth, to shew**
> **himself strong in the behalf of *them***
> **whose heart *is* perfect toward him.**
> **Herein thou hast done foolishly:**
> **Therefore from henceforth thou**
> **shalt have wars.**
> (2 Chronicles 16:9)

My dearer reader, don't let Satan deceive you as he deceived Adam and Eve. No one can fool God. God is greater and larger than all He has created. God is keeping track and records of everything that happens on the earth every second of the day and nothing will escape His watchful eyes. Again, hear what the psalmist says:

Understand, ye brutish among the people: and ye fools, when will ye be wise? He that planted the ear, shall he not hear? he that formed the eye, shall he not see? He that chastiseth the heathen, shall not he correct? he that teacheth man knowledge, shall not he know?
The Lord knoweth the thoughts of man,
(Psalm 94:8-11)

It's Time To Get Re-connected To Your Source.

The objective of God's separation of man from Himself is not for man's destruction. It was humanity that cut itself away from God. The Almighty God does not want to be separated from us, but because of our sin, the separation happened. Sin causes separation from God. Are you also separated from God by your sins? Sin results in separation from God and it eventually produces death—the first death which is the physical death —and then the ultimate separation from God in eternity after which there can never be reconciliation.

Even while they were living outside the Garden of Eden, God never totally abandoned Adam and Eve. The essence of exiling them from their home—the Garden of Eden – was to make them remorseful. God wanted them to repent from their sins. Sadly, today, in the same way, Adam and Eve were separated from God because of their sins, millions, if not billions of people, are today are also exiled from God. They are separated from Him because of their sins. And alas, several millions of people are not even bothered by this separation. They are not remorseful let alone make moves to return to God who is our ONLY source and the Sources of all things. We cannot do well as long as we are cut away from our Source.

Apostle Paul made this known clearly to us in his letter to the early Christians in Corinth:

> **Yet for us there is but one God,**
> **the Father, from whom all things**
> **came and for whom we live;**
> **and there is but one Lord, Jesus**
> **Christ, through whom all things**
> **came and through whom we live.**
> -1 Corinthians 8:6(NIV)

Nehemiah acknowledges the fact that the life we live comes from God. He is the giver of the spiritual life that we lost in the Garden of Eden. The loss of this spiritual life meant calamity and doom for humanity. We all need to return to Him, the Source of our lives:

> "You alone are the LORD You have
> made the heavens, The heaven of
> heavens with all their host, The earth
> and all that is on it, The seas and all
> that is in them You give life to all of
> them And the heavenly host bows
> down before You.
> Nehemiah 9:6

God is eagerly waiting for you and me to return to Him. You can no longer hesitate to take the crucial decision to go back to your Father in heaven who is waiting to receive you back into His arms.

> **2 (For he saith, I have heard thee in a time accepted, and in the day of salvation have I succoured thee: behold, now is the accepted time; behold, now is the day of salvation.)**
> **2 Corinthians 6:2 (KJV)**

Indeed, the same way God expected Adam and Eve to show remorse for their sins, is the same way God is expecting remorse from all sinners today, including anyone reading this book who is yet to give his or her life to Jesus. And for men and women who had known God, who enjoyed His mercy, blessings, favor, power, and glory but went back to their old ways, you need to urgently return to the fold of God because there is no time to waste anymore. The trumpet can sound anytime as preparation for the return of the Lord is in top gear.

God's Invitation To Reconciliation

"And, having made peace through the blood of his cross, by him to reconcile all things unto himself; by him, I say, whether they be things in earth, or things in heaven. And you, that were sometime alienated and enemies in your mind by wicked

works, yet now hath he reconciled In the body of his flesh through death, to present you holy and unblameable and unreproveable in his sight: If ye continue in the faith grounded and settled, and be not moved away from the hope of the gospel, which ye have heard, and which was preached to every creature which is under heaven; whereof I Paul am made a minister; (Col. 1:20–23).

The kernel of the gospel of salvation through faith in Jesus Christ is reconciliation. Since the FIRST coming of our Lord Jesus Christ, God has been at work mending the broken relationship between Him and mankind through His only begotten Son, Jesus Christ. God is every day renewing His friendship or restoring His relationship with mankind. The essence of salvation, which Jesus Christ brought to this world, is reconciliation with God through Jesus Christ, the Lamb of God, and the only one who can renew our relationship with God.

In the Book of John, Jesus Christ left no one in doubt about this truth. He made this very clear. Hear Him:

"I am the way, the truth
and the life, no one comes
to the father but by me"
(John 14:6).

Dear Reader, God is inviting you today to a very important MEETING With Him. He needs your attendance and presence of mind at that meeting which has only ONE single agenda—**the salvation of your soul** through reconciliation with God. The mediator at that meeting is Jesus

Christ. Oh! You are asking for the venue of the meeting? It is right where you are as you are reading this book. It could be in your room, in the bathroom, in your office, or in the car, as you are transiting on a journey from one place to the other. Hear the message God has for you in the Holy Book:

> **And all things are of God, who
> hath reconciled us to himself by
> Jesus Christ, and hath given to
> us the ministry of reconciliation;
> To wit, that God was in Christ,
> reconciling the world unto himself,
> not imputing their trespasses unto
> them; and hath committed unto
> us the word of reconciliation.
> Now then we are ambassadors
> for Christ, as though God did
> beseech you by us: we pray
> you in Christ's stead,
> be ye reconciled to God.**
> . 2 Corinthians 5:18–20

God is earnestly seeking to reconcile you to Himself. And in case you have not accepted Jesus Christ as your personal Lord and savior, you MUST do it at this very moment when you are reading this book.

And, having made peace through the
blood of his cross, by him to reconcile
all things unto himself; by him, I say,
whether they be things in earth, or things
in heaven.
(Col. 1:20).

When you accept Jesus Christ as your personal Lord and savior, it means that you have allowed God to mend His relationship with you which was broken in the Garden of Eden when Adam and Eve ate the forbidden fruit. Consequently, they and their progenies, including you and I, were cut off from God. The Bible says consequent upon Adam's and Eve's sin, mankind---including you and I -- experienced spiritual death—a separation from God. Now, God wants to be reconciled with you and restore your spiritual life.

Do Not Hide Yourself From God Like Adam Did

The Bible told us that immediately Adam and Eve ate the forbidden fruit, their eyes were opened. They instantly knew that they have sinned against God. But rather than approach God for immediate repentance and remedy, they hid themselves from God. When God came looking for Adam, he was not at where God had put him.

Rather than coming to God as a penitent sinner, he hid himself from God. My dear reader, are you not also hiding yourself from God today, even though you can hear his very loud voice calling you to repentance and reconciliation with him through His begotten Son Jesus Christ? God is calling on you today and it is dangerous to ignore His voice:

³ How shall we escape, if we neglect
so great salvation; which at the first
began to be spoken by the Lord,
and was confirmed unto us by
them that
heard him;⁴ God also bearing them
witness, both with signs and
wonders,
and with divers miracles, and
gifts of
the Holy Ghost, according to his
own will
Hebrews 2:3-4 (KJV)

I urge you to heed His call today and be reconciled to Him. Let God end the separation between you and Him occasioned by the Fall of Adam and Eve in the Garden of Eden which He has since remedied through the death of Jesus Christ on the cross because of your sins and the sins of the whole world. You will never regret the decision to accept Jesus Christ into your life and that decision will turn out to be the most important decision of your life.

CHAPTER FIVE

SIN: The Greatest Weapon Of Satan (Our Adversary)

I want to open my message in this chapter with the words of **Watchman Nee** in one of his works: **The Christian Life and Warfare.** Indeed, I believe that every man and woman living on the planet earth, whether born again Christian or not, should take something from Watchman Nee's observation which I considered very crucial to the survival and the achievement of our God-given destinies here on earth.

Nee wants every man and woman on earth that our REAL ENEMY is Satan. Let's hear him:

> **Hence, the most important thing to do now is to clearly identify our enemy. We**

have to know definitely who our enemy
is, who it is that causes us to suffer.
Many times, we think that we have
been taken advantage of by
men. But
the Bible tells us that "our wrestling is
not against blood and flesh but against
the rulers, against the authorities, against
the world-rulers of this darkness, against
the spiritual forces of evil in the heavenlies"
(Eph. 6:12). Hence, every time we suffer at
the hands of men, we have to remember
that behind the men of flesh Satan and his
dark powers are there directing. We

should have the spiritual sight to discern
between God's work and Satan's hidden
schemes. We should differentiate between the natural and the supernatural.
We should be mature and acquire spiritual
knowledge so that nothing of Satan's work
in the dark will escape our observation.

(Collected Works of Watchman Nee, The (Set 1) Vol. 01: The Christian Life and Warfare, Chapter 12, by Watchman Nee)

I agree with Watchman Nee's views on who our enemy is. There is no doubt that our real enemy is Satan And I want to add here that every one of us must know that the greatest weapon the enemy is using against us is **SIN.**The enemy used this weapon against me devastatingly in every area of my life. At every point Satan realized that

I wanted to repent and go back to God, he always strengthened his weapon of sexual immorality he was using against me by making it more lethal such that I will find it difficult to escape. Nevertheless, the merciful God did not fail me. He stretched forth His long arm of deliverance and He rescued me from the hands of Lucifer by His grace. The Almighty Father who was never tired of waiting for me to return to His glorious plans for my life rescued me from worldliness and sin. The Enemy effectively deployed one of his potent weapon in his arsenal—sexual morality— against me to perpetually hold in his cage of sin. Sin indeed caged me.

Sex was the instrument he was using against me to thwart the plan of God for my life and hinder me from fulfilling the purpose why God created me. At a time, when I went back to Nigeria for a brief stay in Benin City for business purposes, ladies were just flocking around me and I enjoyed it. At a point in time, I had nothing less than 10 (ten) women in my life. Women fight themselves because of me and I liked to flaunt my women because the spirit of hedonism had a firm grip on me then. I remember a party that took place in my neighbor's residence, nothing less than seven of my girlfriends attended the party. It was a crazy lifestyle.

However, all through these years of my sexual escapades, God kept reminding me of His plans for my life. He kept sending warnings to me on the need for me, the prodigal son to come back home.I remember two among several of the incidents in which the warnings were given. One day, my white American friend and went to town to catch some fun. On our way back home I picked up a beautiful lady and took her home. After we have enjoyed ourselves it suddenly occurred to me it was time for Bible Study in the church. I told her that I am going out. She asked me where I was heading to and I declared:

"I am going to the church"

"To do what?", she asked me

"To serve God of course"

"God does not need people like you", she told me.

I asked her why she thought God didn't need people like me,

"Oh, you are not fit to serve God. You that are married and yet you are still carrying women, do you think God will accept your service? If you want to serve God, stop dating women, be serious with God and you will be able to serve God". I couldn't controvert her argument, I just gave her some money and left the room.

Another occasion happened in a hotel in Mafoluku area of Lagos Metropolis in Lagos state in Nigeria. On that day, I had invited a female member of our church to the hotel to sleep with her. I warned her to ensure that no member of our church saw her entering the hotel because its location was close to our church. I got to the hotel before her and a few minutes after I settled down in my room, she joined me in the hotel. After we exchange pleasantries, I asked her to join me in the bed but she declined. I was surprised and I asked if she did not know why I brought her to the hotel. She replied and said "yes sir I know but my Jerusalem is not for sale. It is reserved for the man whom I will get married to. He is the one who will disvirgin me". She went on to confess to me that she deliberately accepted my request that she should join me in the hotel because she wanted an opportunity to preach to me. She said she wanted to let me know that I was not serious with God and I needed to give my life to Jesus and begin to serve God.

This lady spent almost an hour preaching to me in the hotel room. I offered her drink and food she rejected them. I gave some money to her she rejected my money. Her behavior shocked me and I never left the hotel room the same way I entered it. Her words had some impact on me and I felt the need to have a change of heart and be serious with God. I realized that I needed to cry out to God for help to save me from sin, the powerful weapon Satan was using to frustrate the purposes of God for my life. Beloved, indeed sin is evil and dangerous. It is a wicked taskmaster that enslaves everyone under its control. Sin is a slave driver and a killer. It has killed so many glorious destinies. Unfortunately millions, if not billions of people, are still toying with this destructive weapon of Satan because they do not know what sin truly is. Therefore beloved reader, at this juncture, before we go further, let us quickly look at what is really called SIN, the three-letter word.

What Is Sin?

In today's 21st Century world, the issue of what constitutes a sin and what does not is generating so much argument within and without the Christendom. Nevertheless, God's standards and his definition of sin have never changed irrespective of the opinions of man. The simple truth is that any thought in our minds which does not conform to the will of God is sin. In the same vein, any action we carry out which is against the will of God is sin. Thus simply put, sin is any thought, utterance, and action which fall below God's standards of holiness.

There is no overemphasizing the fact that our God is a holy God who has holy standards. His standards are perfect and holy. These are the standards which Jehovah God has established all through the ages since He created the heaven and the earth.

Let's Define SIN.

Now, let us critically examine this weapon of the enemy which he used against me for many years in Nigeria and here in the United States to abort the purposes of God for my life. Satan is still using and will continue to use the weapon of sin to separate us from God and destroy our relationship with our Maker until the return of our Messiah, Jesus Christ. Sin is mentioned several times in the Bible. The idea of sin began with the original sin which occurred in the Garden of Eden when Adam and Eve ate of the tree of knowledge. Consequent upon this development, in the words of Apostle Paul, all progenies of Adam and Eve have become sinners. Hear Paul:

> **"Therefore no one will be declared righteous in His sight by observing the law; rather, through the law we become conscious of sin."**
> Romans 3:20

From the foregoing, we can thus describe sin as any action which is against the will of God.

We can also say that any feeling or thought that goes against God's standards is sin. We can also define SIN as an act performed by us, thoughts generated in our minds or utterances made or words spoken by us which result in breaking God's laws. To sum it up, sin is breaking the law of God.

> **Whosoever committeth sin transgresseth**
> **also the law: for sin is the transgression**
> **of the law.** (1 John 3:4; 5:17)

Sins Committed Through Our Thoughts And Utterances

When we engage in sinful thoughts, when we make uncouth utterances and take actions that are unbecoming of children of God, we will end up transgressing against the laws of God. Such behaviors make God unhappy and they are all wrong in the eyes of God. They are unrighteous, behaviors in God's sight. In other words, when unholy thoughts come into our minds, and instead of dismissing them we begin to meditate on them, even before acting on them, we have sinned. Such thoughts are unholy, they are bad and. They are unrighteous in the eyes of God. Indeed, those foul words we speak, the ungodly comments we make, bad jokes, especially lewd ones and criticisms intended to harm another person, all these are sins before God.

Let's hear the Holy Spirit speak on this matter through Apostle Paul:

> **But now you must also rid yourselves**
> **of all such things as these: anger, rage,**
> **malice, slander, and filthy language from your lips.**
> Colossians 3:8

Again in his letter to the Christians in Ephesus, Apostle Paul counseled them thus:

> **⁴ Nor should there be obscenity, foolish talk or coarse joking,**

**which are out of place, but
rather thanksgiving.**
Ephesians 5:4 (NIV)

Sins Committed Through Omission And Commission

As people who want to maintain a relationship with the Holy God, we must be wary of sin in whatever guise or form it comes. Indeed, the Bible talked about sins of omission and sins of commission. All these sins are an abomination unto God. And it is needless to say that they are powerful weapons in the hand of Satan against our lives.

Precisely speaking, sins of commission are those sinful actions that we consciously carried out. When we tell lies, steal or engage proactively in any untoward act we have committed the sin of commission. On the other hand, a sin of omission is a sin that takes place because you do not do somethingthat is right. Examples could include your failure to pray, your failure to be on the side of truth, and indeed failure to witness for Christ.

"So whoever knows the right thing to do
and fails to do it, for him it is sin."
James 4:17

The story told by the Lord Jesus Christ depicts the sin of omission:

> **And Jesus answering said, A certain man went**
> **down from Jerusalem to Jericho, and fell among**
> **thieves, which stripped him of his raiment, and**
> **wounded him, and departed, leaving him half dead.**
> **And by chance there came down a certain priest**
> **that way: and when he saw him, he passed by on**
> **the other side. And likewise, a Levite, when he was**
> **at the place, came and looked on him, and passed**

by on the other side. But a certain Samaritan, as

he journeyed, came where he was: and when he

saw him, he had compassion on him, And went to him,

and bound up his wounds, pouring in oil and wine, and

set him on his own beast, and brought him to an inn,

and took care of him. And on the morrow when he departed,

he took out two pence, and gave them to the host, and said

unto him, Take care of him; and whatsoever thou

spendest more, when I come again, I will repay thee.

Which now of these three, thinkest thou, was neighbour

unto him that fell among the thieves? And he said,

He that shewed mercy on him. Then said Jesus unto

him, Go, and do thou likewise.
(Luke 10:30-37)

From this story, we can see the two men who came upon the injured man, saw the robbery victim in the pool of his own blood and yet failed to help him. Both men passed by without giving helping hands. However, the third man came, stopped and helped the dying man. He knew the right thing to do and he did it. The two men who did not help committed the sin of omission.

In the Book of Mathew, the Lord gave us another scenario of committal of sins of omission. Let's hear the Lord speak:

> **"Then they also will answer, saying, 'Lord, when**
> **did we see you hungry or thirsty or a stranger or**
> **naked or sick or in prison, and did not minister to**
> **you?' Then he will answer them, saying, 'Truly, I**

say to you, as you did not do it to one of the least of these, you did not do it to me.'"
Matthew 25: 44-45

Yet in the Book of First John, we see another example of sins of omission:

"But if anyone has the world's goods and sees
his brother in need, yet closes his heart against
him, how does God's love abide in him? Little
children, let us not love in word or talk but in
deed and in truth." John commanded those
who follow Jesus to live in ways that
show this love to others.
1 John 3:17-18

Also, in the Old Testament, God gave us an insight into how serious the sin of omission is:

"If a person sins in hearing the utterance of an oath, and is a witness, whether he has seen or known of the matter--if he does not tell it, he bears guilt.
Leviticus 5:1(New King James)

Sin And God's Holy Standards

Watchman Nee has helped to pointedly identify our enemy. Whether we like it or not, all human beings on planet earth are engaged in spiritual battle 24/7 with this arch enemy. Usually, the bone of contention in this unending spiritual war of attrition is our relationship with God. As far as God is concerned, our relationship with Him is very important. God is our Creator and the Source of our lives and without Him, we can do nothing as Jesus Christ told us in the Book of John:

**Abide in me, and I in you. As the branch cannot
bear fruit of itself, except it abide in the vine;**

**no more can ye, except ye abide in
me. I am the
vine, ye are the branches: He that
abideth in
me, and I in him, the same bringeth
forth much
fruit: for without me ye can do
nothing. If a man
abide not in me, he is cast forth as
a branch,
and is withered; and men gather
them, and cast
them into the fire, and they are
burned. If ye
abide in me, and my words abide
in you, ye
shall ask what ye will, and it shall
be done unto
you** John 15: 4-7 (KJV).

God does not joke with the relationship He has
with His people. He does not want this relationship
to be broken or destroyed. And this is the reason
He gave us rules we have to follow in walking with

Him. In order to preserve the relationship He has with us, God had to set His standards or rules which will help mankind to enjoy an unbroken relationship with the Holy God. Our God is holy. I dare say that our God, whose name is I AM; I AM THAT I AM,is the ONLY holy God. As a holy God, He cannot tolerate anything evil. Hence, God expects all His creations to also have the nature of holiness.

Indeed when He created Adam and Eve, he gave them holy nature. That was why they could be His very close friends whom He could relate with and spend some time with, in the cool of the day in the Garden of Eden. God set His holy standards for Adam and Eve during their stay in the Garden of Eden. The standards were meant to guide their day-to-day conduct in the Garden of Eden. After God gave them these standards, Adam and Eve obeyed Him perfectly until one day, when Satan came in the form of a serpent into the garden to deceive them.

Satan hated Adam and Eve with perfect hatred because they were not only created in God's image they were also given control, power, and authority over all that God had created. Hence, he vowed to steal their birthright and destroy them, Unfortunately, our first parents eventually could not keep to the divine standards or if you like, laws of God, which the Psalmist described as perfect:

The law of the LORD is perfect, refreshing the soul. The statutes of the LORD are trustworthy, making wise the simple.
Psalm 19:7

Adam and Eve allowed themselves to be deceived by their arch-enemy—Satan--by disobeying God's law. And they fell from the grace of God and the high position in which Jehovah had placed them. Thus sin came into the world through Adam's and Eve's disobedience of God's law.

Your Bad Thoughts, Utterances, And Actions Are Willing Tools In Satan's Hands Against Your Destiny

Dear reader, the simple truth that Satan does not want you to know is that He is using your thoughts, utterances, and actions which do not conform to the will of God to fight against your destiny. Your destiny is God's divine blueprint for your life, the plan of heaven for your life here on earth. Unfortunately, it will be difficult for you to achieve your divine destiny and become what heaven wants you to become on earth if you continue your separation from God through sin.

There is one secret that Satan does not want you to know and that secret is that the **Devil is using your thoughts, utterances, and actions to separate you from your maker.** He wants the separation which began in the Garden of Eden through the sins of Adam and Eve to still continue as far as your relationship with God is concerned. Will you allow the devil to continue to perpetrate this serious harm against your destiny?

Every day, the devil uses his number one weapon—SIN-- against every man and woman on earth to destroy their relationship with God.

Let's look at the following scenarios in the Bible which clearly showed how much Satan hates to see the relationship between God and man to thrive. These scenarios will show you how

Satan has been workingstrenuously all through the ages, up till this very moment you are reading this book, to destroy human beings' destinies.

Scenario One

In the Book of Genesis, Satan worked very hard to turn man against God. Satan told Eve: **"ye shall not surely die"** (Genesis 3:4) whereas God had told Adam and Eve not to eat of the tree of the knowledge of good and evil. **"for in the day that thou eateth thereof, thou shall surely die**. By listening to Satan's lies and obeying the old serpent, the devil succeeded in attacking and destroying the relationship between Adam and Eve and God. What a sad day this was for the whole of the human race. Satan's purpose on planet earth was and still ever remains to kill, to steal, and destroy.

Scenario Two

In the Book of Job, Satan again made serious efforts to turn God against man, this time his focus was Job.

> And the Lord said unto Satan, Hast thou
> considered my servant Job, that there is
> none like him in the earth, a perfect and
> an upright man, one that feareth God,
> and escheweth evil? Then Satan answered
> the Lord, and said, Doth Job fear God for
> nought? Hast not thou made an hedge
> about him, and about his house, and about
> all that he hath on every side? thou hast blessed
> the work of his hands, and his substance is
> increased in the land. But put forth thine hand

now, and touch all that he hath, and he will

curse thee to thy face. And the Lord said unto

Satan, Behold, all that he hath is in thy power;

only upon himself put not forth thine hand.

So Satan went forth from the presence of

the Lord (Job 1:8 KJV)

Scenario Three

Having conquered the FIRST Adam and destroyed the relationship between man and God, Satan spared no effort in waging war against the Redemptive Work of the SECOND Adam—Jesus Christ. He prepared very well and attacked Jesus Christ When Satan thought Jesus Christ was weak---having just finished 40 days marathon Dry Fast and prayers. He went to the wilderness and launched a very subtle but ferocious attack against the Saviour of the world in order to abort God's program of redemption and salvation for man.

And when he had fasted forty days and forty

nights, he was afterward an hungered. And

when the tempter came to him, he said, If

thou be the Son of God, command that these

stones be made bread. But he answered and

said, It is written, Man shall not live by bread

alone, but by every word that proceedeth out of

the mouth of God. Then the devil taketh him

up into the holy city, and setteth him on a pinnacle

of the temple, And saith unto him, If thou be the

Son of God, cast thyself down: for it is written,

He shall give his angels charge concerning

thee: and in their hands they shall bear thee up,

lest at any time thou dash thy foot against a

stone. Jesus said unto him, It is written again,

Thou shalt not tempt the Lord thy God. Again,

the devil taketh him up into an exceeding high

mountain, and sheweth him all the kingdoms

of the world, and the glory of them; And saith

unto him, All these things will I give thee,

if thou wilt fall down and worship me. Then

saith Jesus unto him, Get thee hence,

Satan: for it is written, Thou shalt worship the
Lord thy God, and him only shalt thou serve.
Then the devil leaveth him, and, behold, angels
came and ministered unto him.
Mathew 4:4-11(KJV)

In all the above scenarios, the objective of Satan is to use the instrument of disobedience to break the relationship between God and man. Indeed, God wants us to abide in a relationship with Him. The devil understands this and he is working hard daily to disrupt this relationship

Holiness, The Bulwark Against Sin And Satan

Having understood what constitutes sin and how potent it is in the hand of our major enemy, Satan, what then is the antidote, the neutralizer we can use against sins? Indeed, holiness is an attribute of God. It is His nature. Anything contrary to holiness cannot be found in God. This is also how God wants His people to live on planet earth.

> **"And the Lord spake unto Moses saying, Speak**
> **unto the children of Israel, and say unto them**
> **Ye shall be holy; for I the Lord your God am holy."**
> (Leviticus 19: 1, 2.)

> **"Sanctify yourselves therefore, and be ye holy:**
> **for I am the Lord your God."**
> (Leviticus 20: 7.)
> **"Thou shalt sanctify him therefore; for he offereth**
> **the bread of thy God; he shall be holy unto thee;**
> **for I the Lord, which sanctify you, am holy."**
> (Leviticus 21: 8.)

Dear reader, I need not bore you with academic definitions of holiness and get you confused by what men, especially the so-called experts and theologians considered to be holiness and what holiness is not. Nevertheless, we must know that holiness is a divine attribute of God. God wants us to know that holiness is simply purity, and purity is essential to the Being of God, our Creator. God is pure in His thought, feeling, and deeds. Little wonder He wants us to also separate ourselves from this present evil world and from everything pertaining to it.

Thus in order to be reconnected to God and maintain that connection and build a life-long relationship with Him, we must live a life of holiness within and without (both in our thoughts and in our actions).

The Call To Repentance

In his letter to the people in Corinth, Apostle Paul showed us the path to take when we are ready to return to God.

> **2 (For he saith, I have heard thee
> in a time accepted, and in the day**

of salvation have I succoured thee: behold, now is the accepted time; behold, now is the day of salvation.)
2 Corinthians 6:2 (KJV)

Now is the time for you, dear reader, to embrace Jesus Christ if you have not accepted Him. However, the process of reconciling with God must begin with penitence. You need to admit your sins and recognize yourself as a sinner.

**If we claim to be without sin, we deceive ourselves
and the truth is not in us.9 If we confess our sins, he is
faithful and just and will forgive us our sins and purify
us from all unrighteousness. 10 If we claim we have not sinned,
we make him out to be a liar and his word is not in us.**
1 John 1:8-10 New International Version (NIV)

CHAPTER SIX

God's PlanTo Rescue ManFrom Sin

When God finished His work of creation, the Bible says everything was in a perfect state. It was a good world with good people (Adam and Eve) in it. Our first parents were relating very well with God who has a deep affection for them. They drew their being and everything that pertains to them from God. Jehovah was thelife-sustaining source for Adam and Eve as well as every other thing in the world that He created. For the continuity of this relationship God gave very clear but strict instructions to Adam and Eve which they must follow:

And the Lord God commanded the man, saying, Of every tree of the

garden thou mayest freely eat: But of the tree of the
knowledge of good and evil, thou shalt
not eat of it: for in the day that thou eatest
thereof thou shalt surely die.
Gen. 2:16-17

But man disappointed God. Adam and Eve failed to abide by the instruction of God. They ignored His law which was meant to protect man from evil and instead pandered to the wishes of their arch enemy—Satan.

And he said unto the woman, Yea, hath God
said, Ye shall not eat of every tree of the garden?
And the woman said unto the serpent, We may
eat of the fruit of the trees of the garden: But of
the fruit of the tree which is in the midst of the

garden, God hath said, Ye shall not eat of it,

neither shall ye touch it, lest ye die. And the

the serpent said unto the woman, Ye shall not

surely die: For God doth know that in the day ye

eat thereof, then your eyes shall be opened,

and ye shall be as gods, knowing good and

evil. And when the woman saw that the tree

was good for food, and that it was pleasant

to the eyes, and a tree to be desired to make

one wise, she took of the fruit thereof, and

did eat, and gave also unto her husband with

her; and he did eat. And the eyes of them

both were opened, and they knew
that
they were naked;
Gen. 3:1-7

This incident in the Garden of Eden heralded the entrance of sin into the world:

> **Therefore just as through one man**
> **sin entered**
> **into the world, and through sin,**
> **death; and thus**
> **death passed on to all men because**
> **all have**
> **sinned"**
> Romans 5:12

The "one man" who brought sin and its calamitous consequences to the world was the first man, Adam. He opened the door for Satan and sin to enter into the world and afflict mankind. When Adam partook of the fruits of the tree of knowledge of good and evil, Satan succeeded in bringing sin into the life of man. He brought pollution to mankind.

Consequently, sin affected man's entire being. According to Apostle Paul, sin affected man's entire being – man's body was damaged, man's soul was corrupted, and man's spirit was deadened. As a result, man was no longer in a condition to contact and receive from God as his Source of life. Man could no longer receive spiritual nourishment from Godlike before. Hear Paul in Ephesians 2:1:

> **"And you hath he quickened, who were dead**
> **in trespasses and sins; Wherein in time past**
> **ye walked according to the course of this world,**
> **according to the prince of the power of the air,**
> **the spirit that now worketh in the children of**
> **disobedience.** Ephesians 2:1-2

Thus, instead of God reigning in mankind, and manifesting His glory, Satan and sin were reigning. And the repercussion of this was spiritual and physical death for all men. Man decided to trust the enemy rather than God, his maker, and source. Inevitably, the connection between mankind and his sources was broken. By implications of Adam and Eve's actions, they rejected God's authority, love, and relationship and separated themselves from eternal life which God had given to them when they were created. Humanitythus effectively severed its relationship of love, life-long sustenance, and blessings with God.

The original plan of God for mankind is that man should enjoy everlasting life on the earth. It was however necessary that he prove his character as an obedient steward in charge of all that God has created. There must be obedience to divine lawsand the penalty for disobeying God's laws was and is still death except you are redeemed by the atoning blood of His Son, Jesus Christ.

God stated His law very simply and made it clear to Adam and Eve that the penalty for disobedience is death. But Satan, speaking through the "serpent," said to mother Eve that death would not result from disobeying God's command.—Gen. 3:1-5. Unfortunately, the

inexorable consequence of their disobedience
was both physical and spiritual death.

Unto the woman he said, I will greatly multiply
thy sorrow and thy conception; in sorrow thou
shalt bring forth children; and thy desire shall
be to thy husband, and he shall rule over thee.
And unto Adam he said, Because thou hast
hearkened unto the voice of thy wife, and hast
eaten of the tree, of which I commanded thee,
saying, Thou shalt not eat of it: cursed is the
ground for thy sake; in sorrow shalt thou eat
of it all the days of thy life; Thorns also and

thistles shall it bring forth to thee; and thou
shalt eat the herb of the field; In the sweat
of thy face shalt thou eat bread, till thou return
unto the ground; for out of it wast thou taken
: for dust thou art, and unto dust shalt
thou Return Genesis 3:16-19

Their punishment became inevitable because God's goodness and justice require a judgment against evil in all forms and humanity now seems to be bound to that ultimate fate--eternal life in Hell-fire except there is the shedding of a holy blood which can take away the sins which Adam and Eve have committed.

> [22] **And almost all things are by the law purged with blood; and without shedding of blood is no remission. Hebrews 9:22 (KJV)**

Emmanuel S. Omere

The Promise Of God's Redemption For All Mankind

The love of God for the human race is infinite. God demonstrated this love when He instantaneously pronounced a program of redemption for mankind even on the very day Adam and Eve fell from Grace. Yes, the same moment on the same day Godpronounced His judgment upon them and drove Adam and Eve out of the Garden of Eden, on the account of their transgression against His holy law, that same day and moment God announced a plan to rescue them from eternal perdition, or eternal punishment and damnation into which a sinful and unrepentant person passes after death.

> **And I will put enmity between thee and the woman, and between thy seed and her seed; it shall bruise thy head, and thou shalt bruise his heel.** Gen. 3:15

Dear reader, this promise of God is for you

and I. The promise is intended to rescue us from eternal damnation. God promised to send a Saviourto the world, a Saviour who will redeem us from our sin. Of a truth, we have done evil in more ways than we can comprehend.

As it is written, There is none righteous, no,

not one: There is none that understandeth,

there is none that seeketh after God. They

are all gone out of the way, they are together

become unprofitable; there is none that doeth

good, no, not one. Their throat is an open

sepulchre; with their tongues they have

used deceit; the poison of asps is under

their lips: Whose mouth is full of cursing and

> **bitterness: Their feet are swift to shed blood:**
> **Destruction and misery are in their ways:**
> **And the way of peace have they not known:**
> **There is no fear of God before their eyes.**
> Rom 3:10-18

Unfortunately for you and me, we cannot, in our power, rescue ourselves from this calamitous situation. Indeed, our thoughts, utterances are intrinsically evil. Mankind is emotionally and spiritually addicted to evil. Though he loves us, God must and will judge all our evil thoughts, words, and deeds. His wrath including eternal imprisonment in Hell Fire for unrepentant sinners is real and justified.

> **And I saw a great white throne, and him that sat**
> **on it, from whose face the earth and the heaven**
> **fled away; and there was found no place for them.**

And I saw the dead, small and great, stand before

God; and the books were opened: and another

book was opened, which is the book of life: and

the dead were judged out of those things which

werewritten in the books, according to their works.

And the sea gave up the dead which were in

it; and death and hell delivered up the dead which

were in them: and they were judged every man

according to their works. And death and hell were

cast into the lake of fire. This is the second death.

And whosoever was not found written in the book

of life was cast into the lake of fire.
Rev 20:11-15.

Emmanuel S. Omere

God's Rescue Plan For Your Life

My dear reader, do you know that God is interested
in your soul? Yes, He is! Ever since God formed
you in your mother's womb, He has known you
and everything about you. Indeed, God has a
blueprint for your life. He wanted—and indeed
has always wanted—you to succeed in life so that
you can show forth His glory. But alas, Satan and
your sins are always ready to hinder you. For so
long you have been suffering theconsequences
ofyour sins.When you tell lies, steal, cheat, or
deceive others, all these sinful acts are directed
at God Himself, thereby making Him unhappy.

The person you offended the most by these
actions was GOD Himself.

**Now the works of the flesh are
manifest,
which are these; Adultery,
fornication,
uncleanness, lasciviousness,
Idolatry,
witchcraft, hatred, variance,
emulations,**

130

wrath, strife, seditions, heresies, Envyings,
murders, drunkenness, revellings, and such
like: of the which I tell you before, as I have
also told you in time past, that they which
do such things shall not inherit the kingdom
of God. Galatians 5:19-21

You and I have the depraved human nature that is susceptible to sin. That is why we easily commit sin. But God is ready to help you out of this quagmire. The transgression of Adam and Eve in the Garden of Eden and the concomitant punishment, came long before they began to give birth to children. And by the time they gave birth to Cain, Abel, and other children, their punishment had already gone into effect.

The effects of God's sanctions on them and their depraved nature which replaced the perfect and holy nature they got when created them, had manifested. Hence, all their children, and by implications, all human beings that came through them, including you and I, shared in their punishment and their depraved nature. Instead of holy nature, we wereborn withimperfect nature that is vulnerable to sin. And like our first parents, we too automatically came under condemnation to death.

> **Wherefore, as by one man sin entered into the**
> **world, and death by sin; and so death passed**
> **upon all men, for that, all have sinned: (For until**
> **the law sin was in the world: but sin is not imputed**
> **when there is no law. Nevertheless, death reigned**
> **from Adam to Moses, even over them, that had**
> **not sinned after the similitude of Adam's transgression,**

**who is the figure of him that was
to come**
Rom. 5:12-14

Thus the of effects of God's judgment of **Death For Sin**, which is the repercussion for Adam's and Eve's disobedience, have continued to work on mankind all through the ages. Today, several millions of people worldwide are still suffering and will continue to suffer the consequences of Adam's and Eve's sins. Among these are sorrow, oppression by Satan, enslavement to sin, sickness, as well as pain—mental and physical— being experienced by all, both young and old, in every generation. The only way out is to come to Jesus Christ the only Person who has power over Satan and Sin. Only Jesus can deliver you from the bondage of sin in which you are now as a result of Adam's and Eve's sins and your own sins too. Do not tarry any longer come to Him today.

In the Book of Romans, Apostle Paul described these sufferings as *"the wrath of God (which) is revealed from heaven against all ungodliness and unrighteousness."* (Rom. 1:18).

The Bible also warned us that Godwill judge all our sins. Apostle Paul speaks further in the Book of Romans:

> **23for all have sinned and fall short**
> **of the glory**
> **of God, 24and all are justified**
> **freely by his grace**
> **through the redemption that came**
> **by Christ**
> Roman3: 23-24

But thanks be to God for His promise of redemption through Jesus Christ His only begotten Son.

Jesus Christ's Work Of Redemption

God's eternal plan of salvation for man can never be nullified by Satan even though Satan's ultimate objective is to frustrate and destroy God's plan. God in His infinite wisdom will always achieve His purpose in heaven and on the earth no matter what happens. And so for God to carry out His original rescue plan for man, He shocked Satan when He decided to come down to the earth and died for man since the penalty for Adam's and Eve's sin is death which must take place.

So, about two thousand years ago, God who created the heaven and the earth, became a man, born with Holy blood flowing in His veins through a woman---Mary. That Man, the second Adam, was Jesus Christ. Jesus was born in Bethlehem in Israel with the likeness of the flesh of sin like you and I. However, unlike the depraved sinful nature of Adam and Eve, which they transferred to mankind, Jesus Christ's nature was the perfect holy nature of God.

> **³ For what the law was powerless to do because it was weakened by the flesh,[a]God did by sending his own Son in the likeness of sinful flesh to be a sin offering.[b] And so he condemned sin in the flesh, but our Lord without the sinful nature (Rom. 8:3).**
> Romans 8:3 (NIV)

Jesus Christ of Nazareth was sent by God the Father, out of love, into the world on a mission to rescue men and women. In obedience to God's plan Jesus lived a sinless life, yet He willingly gave up His life and died on a cross to rescue you and me. By his death and resurrection three days later, Jesus broke the power of sin and death. After He rose from the dead, Jesus was seen alive again by hundreds of people.

Dear reader, you can confirm God's readiness to die a shameful death in order to rescue you and me and the rest of humanity in the Book of John. His coming to this world to die on the Crossto execute His rescue program was explained by the writer of that Gospel:

> **In the beginning was the Word, and the Word was with God, and the Word was God. ²He was in the beginning with God. ³All things were made through Him, and without Him nothing was made that was made. ⁴In Him was life, and the life was the light of men. ⁵And the light shines in the darkness, and the darkness did**

not comprehend[a] it. ¹⁴ And the Word became flesh and dwelt among us, and we beheld His glory, the glory as of the only begotten of the Father, full of grace and truth.¹⁵ John bore witness of Him and cried out, saying, "This was He of whom I said, 'He who comes after me is preferred before me, for He was before me.'"
John 1-5; 14-15 (NKJV)

God became a man because of you. That man, the Second Adam, Jesus Christ lived and walked on this planet earth for thirty-three and half years at the end of which He died on the cross for your sins and my sins.

**"In whom we have redemption through His blood,
the forgiveness of offenses,
according to the riches
of His grace"** Ephesians 1:7

Emmanuel S. Omere

Through His death on a cross, Jesus paid the price for your sin and mine. The Bible says:

**"But God demonstrates his own
love for us in this: While we were**

The simple reason why you cannot afford to ignore the wonderful offer of salvation for your soul which Jesus Christ is extending to you as you are reading this book is that the Lord Jesus gave himself up as a sacrifice on your behalf. He died in your place on the cross. The death you should have died as a result of the lies you have been telling; the punishment of death for all kinds of sins, the work of your flesh, Jesus bore this painful punishment on your behalf.

**[19] Now the works of the flesh
are evident, which are: adultery,
[a] fornication, uncleanness,
lewdness, [20] idolatry, sorcery,
hatred, contentions, jealousies,
outbursts of wrath, selfish
ambitions, dissensions,
heresies, [21] envy, murders,**

[b]**drunkenness, revelries, and**
thelike; of which I tell you
beforehand, just as I also told
you **in time past, that those**
who practice such things will
not inherit the kingdom of God.
Galatians 5:19-21 (NKJV)

For all your sins and mine, Jesus Christ took upon himself God's punishment that our sins deserve. But glory be to God because Jesus Christ is now alive forevermore and sits at the right hand of God the Father in Heaven, in a place of glory and honor. Are you ready to accept God's rescue plan for your life? Do you want Jesus to rescue you from your sins and your present way of life? If you reject this plan, then it means that the punishment of Death For Sin will still be carried out by God against you. And you have no way of escape except you accept Jesus Christ.

[23] **For the wages of sin is death;**
but the gift of God is eternal life
through Jesus Christ our Lord.
Romans 6:23 King James Version (KJV)

Dear reader, the GOOD NEWS is that God is - even now - ready, willing and able to forgive your sins and remove that separation which began in the Garden of Eden and which Satan and sin have elongated. This forgiveness by God restores the opportunity for you to once again reconnect to your maker so that you can have a loving relationship with God your creator. Are you prepared to turn from your present way of life, change your direction and turn to God your creator for a fresh start? If you choose to call upon Jesus to save you, He will set you free, give you eternal life and a place in God's family.

Jesus Christ was sinless, yet He paid the price due for your sin - in your place. Now, you can put your trust in Him to save you. He is the propitiation for the sins of the whole world. You can trust in Him as your substitute and consequently go free. So you do not have to suffer the repercussions for by our own sins anymore because of what Jesus has done. After putting your trust in Jesus to save you, God will then give you the power to overcome sin and you will begin to live a new life:

"For it is by grace you are saved, through faith, and this not of yourselves; it is the gift of God, so that none can boast".

God offers you His forgiveness as a free gift. Through the death of Christ all your sins, my own sins, and that of the whole world were forgiven and washed away. And since the penalty of sin that Adam and Eve committed, which they all also transmitted to all human beings was death, the Second Adam, Jesus Christ had to **PAY THIS PRICE** by dying on the cross of Calvary.

CHAPTER SEVEN

Salvation: The Priceless Gift From God

The salvation of the soul of a man is priceless. It is inestimable and incomparable with anything of high value. Salvation is worth more than trillions of US Dollars. The redemption of the soul of man was achieved via the shedding of the Blood of Jesus Christ on the cross at Calvary. It takes a dirty and a chronic sinner like me, who experienced God's FREE salvation and was consequently rescued by God's matchless grace at the gate of HELL FIRE, to really appreciate the worth of salvation achieved by the Lamb of God who was made the propitiation of our sins.

Unfortunately, a lot of Christians today do not know the worth or value of the grace they have received from God, courtesy of the FINISHED WORK OF REDEMPTION on the cross at Calvary. I thank God for His grace upon my life. I am a fortunate sinner whofound uncommon mercy and favor in the eyes of the Lord. He saved my soul from destruction and by His mercy, He rescued me from the bondage of sin and its dire repercussions. The Lord gave me liberty and dominion power over sin.What is more, I have enjoyed and still enjoying the benefits of the genuine salvation that comes through the blood of Jesus Christ. Part of these benefits is the acquittal of my daughter in a case that could have resulted in her being jailed for 21 years. The mercy of God set her free. Again, Godcanceled the verdict of death given to me by top Cancer specialist doctors at Boston Cancer MedicalCentre, who gave me just three months to live on planet earth before I die from chronic Cancer ailment.

It is rather unfortunate that in spite of the high value of salvation, not every man or woman sees salvation as an important thing they must seek for. Nonetheless, whether we believe it or not, what is of greatest importance to God is the salvation of the soul of man. That was why God gave us Jesus Christ His only begotten Son. In the Book of John, the Bible declared thus:

> **For God so loved the world that He gave**
> **His only begotten Son that whosoever**
> **believeth in Him should not perish, but have**
> **everlasting life. (John 3:16 KJV)**

Again, in his message to early Christians, Apostle Jude has this to say about the importance of our salvation and our faith in the Lord Jesus Christ:

> **Beloved, while I was making every effort to**
> **write you about our common salvation,**
> **I was compelled to write to you (urgently)**
> **appealing that you fight strenuously for**

(the defense of)the faith which was once
for all handed down to the saints,the faith that
is the sum of Christian belief that was given
verbally to believers (Jude 1:3 AMP)

It is rather unfortunate that many people today are just church goers. They do not know the reason why God ordered us to congregate in His presence as a church. The essence of going to the church—which is the salvation of our souls—is lost on them. More or less they are playing with their destinies and their eternity. This reminds me of the case of one of my brothers who toyed with the salvation of his soul. This person is my blood relation. He really got a raw deal from Satan on account of his lack of seriousness with the salvation of his soul.In the Book of Psalm the Bible declared thus:

He that dwelleth in the secret place of the Most

High shall abide under the shadow of the Almighty.
I will say of the Lord He is my refuge and my fortress:
my God; in Him will I trust (Psalm 91:1-2)

The first attack launched by Satan against my brother was aimed at his marriage. The enemy engineered the manipulation of his marriage and Satansucceeded because there was no Christ in his life. My brother was not saved; he was not in the secret place of God and when the enemy came, he couldn't hide under the shadow of theAlmighty. He never believed in the LordJesus Christ.

Although he got married to the woman of his choice whom he had been in love with while in the United States, yet the enemy—Satan—still struck against his marriage and disorganized his marital life. At a point in time, he had to leave the United States for Nigeria. On getting home, Satan manipulated him and he got married to another woman. That marriage produced three children but it didn't last. It broke down and they had to pack it up. Nevertheless, the woman vowed that as long she is alive, my brother will never succeed in marrying another woman, no matter how hard he tried.

Unfortunately, until today, my brother iswithout a wife. There was a time he was seriously ill. I went to the hospital and preached to him. I prayed with him as well as gave him some books to read. He got healed and even came to our church to give testimony. But sadly, today, he is back in the world, he has exited the fold of Christ.

What Does Salvation Means

There is hardly any word that is so much being bandied about every day in the Christendom like the word *salvation*. Perhaps another word that has a high frequency of use and mention, like salvation, is '**born-again**'. Oftentimes we hear people ask questions such as: "have you been saved?" On many occasions, we've heard the preacher say "please be saved". Can we then conclude that because of its frequent usage everyone is cleared about the meaning of salvation? And dear reader, looking at the issue from a personal level, what sense can you make of the word SALVATION as far as your life here on earth and in the world to come is concerned?In a simple term, from the perspective of a Christian, we can explain the meaning of salvation in two ways:

1. To save a person from danger
2. To save a person from the punishment he or she duly deserves.

So, basically, within the context of the first sense of the meaning of the word salvation, it means 'deliverance' or to deliver a person from danger. This type of deliverance is the kind of rescue given to a person at the risk of peril, it means saving or rescuing such a person from an inevitable danger. To understand what I am talking about here, let's quickly go back to that great spectacle that occurred at the Red Sea in Egypt and we can see the practical demonstration of the word salvation. It is a great occurrence, the type that had had never been witnessed in the world before and the type of which, since then, has never been replicated.

**And Moses said unto the people,
Fear ye not, stand**

**still, and see the salvation of the
Lord, which he will**

**shew to you to day: for the
Egyptians whom ye have**

**seen to day, ye shall see them
again no more for ever.**

**The Lord shall fight for you, and ye
shall hold**

**your peace. And the Lord said unto
Moses, Wherefore**

**criest thou unto me? speak unto
the children of Israel,**

**that they go forward: But lift thou
up thy rod, and**

**stretch out thine hand over the
sea, and divide it: and**

**the children of Israel shall go on
dry ground through**

the midst of the sea
Exodus 14:15-16

And just imagine this great scene, an awesome display of God's mighty power"

> **And Moses stretched forth his hand over the**
> **sea, and the sea returned to his strength**
> **when the morning appeared; and the Egyptians**
> **fled against it; and the Lord overthrew the**
> **Egyptians in the midst of the sea. And the**
> **waters returned, and covered the chariots, and**
> **the horsemen, and all the host of Pharaoh that**
> **came into the sea after them; there remained**
> **not so much as one of them. But the children**
> **of Israel walked upon dry land in the midst of the**

sea; and the waters were a wall unto them on

their right hand, and on their left. Thus the Lord

saved Israel that day out of the hand of the

Egyptians; and Israel saw the Egyptians dead

upon the sea shore. And Israel saw that great

work which the Lord did upon the Egyptians:

and the people feared the Lord, and believed

the Lord, and his servant Moses

Exodus 14:27-31

That was a quintessential practical demonstration of the meaning of the word salvation. In this context of the meaning of salvation, God physically deployed His power to deliverthe children of Israel from the armies of Egyptians.

Saved From Punishment

However, there is another sense of the meaning of the word salvation. That is the second sense as explained above, i..e being saved from due punishment. In the light of the focus of our discourse from the preceding chapters, salvation in this sense would mean saving or rescuing a person from the penalty or repercussions of his or her sins which he or she has committed.

The fellow that is saved from punishment will no doubt deserves the punishment which is a consequence of an offense he or she duly deserves.

Now, let's look at the meaning of salvation, as it relates to escaping punishment, and here we are talking about escaping from the punishment of God which is **DEATH FOR SIN.** God's divine and just instruction to Adam and Eve is that:

But of the tree of the knowledge of good and evil, thou shalt
not eat of it: for in the day that thou eatest

thereof thou shalt surely die.
Gen. 2:16-17

In the above instruction, a divine decree was issued. "**For in the day that thou eatestthereof thou shalt surely die**". And following Adam and Eve's disobedience,**DEATH FOR SIN** became the lot of humanity. Salvation, in this context, would then mean the deliverance of humanity from the penalty of Adam's and Eve's sin of disobedience which is eternal death.

> **For the wages of sin is death; but the gift**
> **of God is eternal life through Jesus Christ**
> **our Lord.** (Romans 6:23).

In Hebrews chapter two verse three, Apostle Paul called it "great salvation". Hear him:

> **How shall we escape, if we neglect so great**
> **salvation; which at the first began to be spoken**

**by the Lord, and was confirmed unto us by them
that heard him; God also bearing them witness,
both with signs and wonders, and with divers
miracles, and gifts of the Holy Ghost, according to
his own will?**Hebrew 2:3(KJV).

Do I Need Salvation?

Dear reader, one of the issues that may be agitating your mind, as you read this book is: why should anyone bother you with the issue of salvation since you are not at the risk of any physical danger and neither are you on trial in court or even imprisoned. If none of the above is happening to you why then should anyone trouble you about the need for you to be saved? Well, the truth of the matter is that you really need salvation and you do not need to be simplistic about this matter.

If you have been following our discourse from

chapter one of this book, it will by now not be difficult for you to know why you need salvation. Yes, indeed, you need to be saved. And the question you are likely to ask is "Why do I need to be saved?" And the answer is found in what happened in the Garden of Eden while Adam and Eve were in the Garden living a life of opulence but under the strict guidance of God:

> **And the Lord God commanded the man, saying,**
> **Of every tree of the garden thou mayest freely**
> **eat: But of the tree of the knowledge of good**
> **and evil, thou shalt not eat of it: for in the day**
> **that thou eatest thereof thou shalt surely die**
> Genesis 2:16-17

However, a monumental tragedy occurred to humanity in the Garden and Eden on account of Satan's attack against man and the fall of Adam and Eve to Satan's deception. The folly of

Adam and Eve brought calamitous consequences to man:

> **And unto Adam he said, Because thou hast**
>
> **hearkened unto the voice of thy wife, and**
>
> **hast eaten of the tree, of which I commanded**
>
> **thee, saying, Thou shalt not eat of it: cursed**
>
> **is the ground for thy sake; in sorrow shalt**
>
> **thou eat of it all the days of thy life; Thorns**
>
> **also and thistles shall it bring forth to thee;**
>
> **and thou shalt eat the herb of the field; In the**
>
> **sweat of thy face shalt thou eat bread,**
>
> **till thou return unto the ground; for out of it**

wast thou taken: for dust thou art, and unto
dust shalt thou return. Genesis 3:17-19

Adam and Eve were warned by God in Genesis chapter two against eating the forbidden fruits. By the time we got to chapter three, we found out that Adam and Eve, the first pair of human beings, had disobeyed God. The punishment for their sin, as God had earlier on warned, is death:

for in the daythat thou eatest thereof
thou shalt surely die

The death God talked about is in two folds:

1. Spiritual death
2. Physical Death.

In the Book of Ezekiel, God through His prophet expatiate this matter very well:

"Behold all souls are Mine; the soul
of the father,

as well as the soul of the son is
Mine; the soul who
sins shall die"
(Ezekiel 18:4).

Again in verse 20, the Lord emphasized this
punishment of *Death For Sin*:

The soul that sinneth, it shall die.
The son
shall not bear the iniquity of the
father, neither
shall the father bear the iniquity of
the son: the
righteousness of the righteous
shall beupon
him, and the wickedness of the
wicked shall be
upon him. But if the wicked will
turn from all
his sins that he hath committed,
and keep all my
statutes, and do that which is
lawful and right, he

**shall surely live, he shall not die.
All his transgressions
that he hath committed, they shall
not be mentioned
unto him: in his righteousness that
he hath done he
shall live.** (Ezekiel 18:20)

Dear reader, this punishment of **DEATH FOR SIN** applies to all human beings who are progenies of Adam and Eve. You and I cannot escape it. It is a divine punishment that no one, including you and I, cannot escape. We must bear the consequences of Adam's and Eve's sins and the punishment for the sins we have committed or still committing. IF YOU DO NOT ACCEPT JESUS CHRIST AS YOUR LORD AND SAVIOUR, you will be punished by God. In the book of Romans, God made this very clear through Apostle Paul:

**"For all have sinned and fall short
of the glory
of God"** (Romans 3:23).

**"For the wages of sin is death, but
the gift of
God is eternal life in Christ Jesus
our Lord"
(Romans 6:23).**

From the foregoing, you can now see, dear reader, that the word salvation makes great meaning to you and I if we really want to escape the divine punishment of DEATH FOR SIN. Indeed, every man and woman needs to be saved or delivered from eternal death. And wait for this--- after the deliverance, you will get an important PRIZE, a FREE GIFT from God. That free gift is the prevention of your soul from dying as a result of your sin, in accordance with the words of Prophet Ezekiel. Rather than dying in HELL-FIRE which is the right outcome of DEATH FOR SIN punishment, you will be granted eternal life in paradise with God THROUGH Jesus Christ. Now, dear reader, you can now see why salvation is necessary. Indeed, that is why JesusChrist came to the earth in the form of a human being.

**"For the Son of Man has come to seek and
to save that which was lost" (Luke 19:10).**

It was the death of Jesus Christ on the cross that fulfilled the requirement of the divine punishment of **DEATH FOR SIN**. Your salvation and mine is only possible because of the great sacrifice of Jesus Christmade on the cross.

Let's listen to Apostle Paul:

> **"But God demonstrates His own love toward us, in that while we were yet sinners, Christ died for us."**
> Romans 5:8

Jesus Christ chose to die for you and I. He knew no sin, but He was used as the sacrificial Lamb for your sins and mine. He gave His life, a life of perfection, without sin, for us and the rest of humanity so that we can be saved. The basis of your salvation and mine salvation from God's punishment is simply the fact that **we accept**

Jesus Christ's sacrifice on the cross as true and real. Our salvation is also possible because we believe that Jesus Christ's blood that wasshed on the cross when He was crucified took away the sins of the whole world. Dear reader, this is the truth and nothing but the truth that thesalvation of the whole world was made possible by the death of Jesus Christ on the cross.

The ABC Of Salvation

The issue of salvation is as simple as ABC. The Lord Jesus Christ has made it very simple for you and I on the account of what He did on the cross. The redemptive work of our Saviour on the cross has opened the door of salvation for us. Having understood the meaning of the word salvation and how it applies to you and I, then when need to take concrete action which will bring it to effect in our lives as Moses did at the Red Sea when He obeyed God's simple instruction to stretch his Rod on the Red Sea and salvation was effected in the lives of children of Israel who were saved from their enemies.

In the same vein, you and I need to be saved from our enemies---Satan and Sin. We need to accept the sacrifice of Jesus Christ on the Cross of Calvary. Just as God instructed Moses at the Red Sea, on what to be done so that he and the children of Israel could be saved, Gods is also giving you and I the instruction on what to do so that we could be saved from sin and Satan.

In the Book of Isaiah there is an instruction for you and I which we must carry out:

> **"Seek the LORD while He may be found, call**
> **upon Him while He is near. Let the wicked**
> **forsake his way, and the unrighteous man his**
> **thoughts; let him return to the LORD, and He will**
> **have mercy on him; and to our God, for He will**
> **abundantly pardon"**
> (Isaiah 55:6-7).

The following are the three ABC steps you need to take to carry out this instruction from God:

The AOf Salvation: Admit
You Are A Sinner

Apostle Paul made it clear that all of us are guilty and no one can get himself or herself exonerated from blame. Hence, you need to admit that you are a sinner who needs the saving grace of God. Again listen to Apostle Paul:

> **For all have sinned and fall short of the glory**
> **of God"(Romans 3:23). "For the wages of sin is**
> **death, but the gift of God is eternal life in Christ**
> **Jesus our Lord" (Romans 6:23).**

The B Of Salvation: Believe That Christ Jesus Is the Son Of God

After admitting that you are a sinner who deserves to be punished, you need to recognize the fact that you cannot help yourself; on your own, there is no escaping from the just punishment from the righteous God. You need a savior who will save you from sin and its consequence which is the SECOND DEATH IN HELL-FIRE. Here lies the kernel of the issue of salvation because about two thousand years ago, Someone, the second Adam, has paid the price for your sin. He had stood in the gap for you by dying on the cross instead of you. All you need to do now is to believe all the works Jesus Christ did on the cross.

The C Of Salvation: Confess Christ Jesus As You Lord And Savior

Having believed Jesus Christ as the son of God and accepted His finished work on the cross, the next step to take is to open your mouth and confess Him as your personal Lord and Saviour.

thatof your soul, He owns us in two folds, one by the creation and secondly by redemption.

> **That if you confess with your mouth the**
> **Lord Jesus and believe in your heart that**
> **God has raised Him from the dead, you will**
> **be saved. ¹⁰ For with the heart one believes**
> **unto righteousness, and with the mouth**
> **confession is made unto salvation.**
> **¹¹ For the Scripture says, "Whoever believes on**
> **Him will not be put to shame." ¹²**
> **For there is**
> **no distinction between Jew and Greek, for the**
> **same Lord over all is rich to all who call upon Him**
> Romans 10:9-12 New King James Version (NKJV)

Your Salvation Experience

Every day we go through many experiences as we grow and develop physically and spiritually. Some of these experiences help us to become better persons as they equip us with knowledge, skills and power we need to achieve our purposes on earth. Many of these experiences are good while many are not pleasant. The important thing however is that these experiences are major ingredients of life. Also, some of these experiences are more important than others. Among these crucial and indispensable experiences is the salvation experience.

Indeed, salvation experience is one of the most important life experiences that a person has to go through in life. A person's destiny cannot be fulfilled without having this life-changing experience. And talking about salvation here, I mean salvation in the Christian sense we have earlier explained. Indeed, the Christian doctrine of salvation is a spiritual experience. The very fact that you experience being saved from your sins is a product of your personal encounter with the Lord Jesus Christ.

In most cases, if not all, the experience of salvation is subjective and oftentimes not objective. It is apersonal experience that verbal communicationcannot be enough to explain. Nevertheless, it is a wonderful experience every man and woman, boy and girl, must have. When a person has salvation experience, so much will happen to that person. And one of the things that will happen is that the person's life will be transformed spiritually, physically, materially, and in other ramifications.

A Christian'ssalvation experience begins withhis or her conversion from being a sinner to a child of God. At that stage, you are being "Born Again." At the conversion stage,you are now a saved person who will undergo the spiritual transformation process, courtesy of the Holy Spirit, the Spirit of Jesus Christ. As you go through the transformational process you will slowly be changed into the image of Christ. This will enable you to live a new life in Christ:

17 Therefore if any man be in Christ, he
is a new creature: old things are passed
away; behold, all things are become new
2 Corinthians 5:17 (KJV)

Dear reader, when you become a NEW CREATURE in Jesus Christ, then you will be empowered by the Holy Spirit to live a life that is devoid of sin. The Holy Spirit will empower you to live a life that will make you to conform to the image of Christ.

Behold, what manner of love the Father
hath bestowed upon us, that we should
be called the sons of God: therefore the
world knoweth us not, because it knew him
not. Beloved, now are we the sons of God,

Emmanuel S. Omere

> **and it doth not yet appear what we shall be:**
> **but we know that, when he shall appear, we**
> **shall be like him; for we shall see him as he is.**
> **And every man that hath this hope in him**
> **purifieth himself, even as he is pure.**
> 1 John 3:1-3 (KJV)

Then, at that point, every trace of sin and the flesh in your life, the depraved human nature you and I inherited from Adam and Eve, will be gone. You will no longer inhabit sinful flesh but be directed and guided by the Holy Spirit.

> **For if ye live after the flesh, ye shall die:**
> **but if ye through the Spirit do mortify the**
> **deeds of the body, ye shall live. For as**

many as are led by the Spirit of God, they

are the sons of God. For ye have not received

the spirit of bondage again to fear; but ye

have received the Spirit of adoption, whereby

we cry, Abba, Father. The Spirit itself beareth

witness with our spirit, that we are the

children of God: And if children, then heirs;

heirs of God, and joint-heirs with Christ; if so

be that we suffer with him, that we may be

also glorified to

CHAPTER EIGHT

Working Out Your Salvation

There are so many things that people considered to be great fun and enjoyment in this world. However, In reality, they are no enjoyment. The worldly pleasures are nothing but satanic bait designed to entrap men and women in Satanic bondages. In 1Timothy chapter 5 verse 6, Apostle Paul declared thus:

> **Whereas she (and he too) who lives in pleasures**
> **and self-gratification(giving herself up to luxury and self-indulgence) is dead even when while she (still) lives (1Timothy 5:6 AMP)**

Yes, to indulge in the worldly pleasure of adultery, fornication, womanizing, alcoholism and all kinds of sinful pleasures is to subject oneself to servitude under Satan. However, once anyone surrenders his or her life to Jesus Christ, those so-called worldly pleasures will no longer be meaningful to such a person. They will become so much obnoxious to him or her. And the reason for that person's new disposition is that all those old ways of life which were hitherto pleasant to the person will now be adversative to the person's NEW WAY of life. Yes, such a person, who is now a new person, a new man or new woman in Christ, will now be living and walking in a NEW WAY. That NEW WAY is Jesus Christ.

In this regard, I have a personal experience of having to turn my back on some indulgences, worldly pleasures which hitherto were my pastime. They were sources of pleasure and enjoyment for me but which I now found repugnant and despicable because God loathes them.

Before I came to the US, I had a girlfriend back home in Nigeria when I was still in the world. For a very long time, we lost contact. Later, she too relocated to London. Sometimes ago, she got to know that I am now living in Boston in the United States. She also learned that I have become an evangelist for Jesus Christ. One day she called me and informed me that she is coming to the US to visit her brother in Atlanta. She said after visiting her brother in Atlanta, she would come over to Boston to spend a day or two before going back to London. When I heard about her plan, I wasn't too comfortable with it because I was living alone because my wife was still in Nigeria and it is not proper for me to allow a former girlfriend to stay with me even for two days in the same apartment. Indeed I remember the advice of Apostle Paul to the early Christians in 1Thessalonians 5:22 that we must " abstain from all appearance of evil"

After giving her proposed visit a thought, I called her and told her that I will prefer to send some gifts to her while in Atlanta instead of her coming to visit me in Boston. But the lady insisted on coming to Bostonbecause she said that was how she routed her ticket. I then realized that I have in my hand a delicate situation that I needed to handle with the wisdom of God. So, I thought about what to do. I quickly evaluated the situation and concluded that I could not afford to disappoint her but at the same time, I had to be extremely careful. I realized that the enemy was setting a trap for me. The issue is could this woman stay with me, just two of us in the same apartment for three days without anything happening? I saw the danger to my salvation and what the plan of the enemy is. So, I concluded to act very fast even as I concurred that she can visit me in Boston.

On arrival in Boston, I went to the Airport to pick her up and instead of bringing her to my house I took her to a hotel I had already booked for her. The hotel was not too far from where I live and she stayed in the hotel for four days. On the first day of her visit, I was with her in the hotel for some time. But rather than stay with her in her hotel room, I chose to be with her in an open place within the hotel premises where we could reminisce as well as talk about things happening to us now. During our discussions, I steered our discourse to the issue of salvation and Jesus Christ and after some time I took my leave and left her in the hotel. On the last day of her visit, which was Sunday, we went on shopping, I shopped for her, bought a lot of gifts for her and thereafter took her to my house to know where I live. When she got to my house, she discovered that I was living alone. She now asked me why I had to lodge her in a $150 per night hotel for her when I could easily have accommodated her in my apartment. She said why should I just waste about $500 on hotel accommodation for her instead of allowing her to stay with me? I told her that it was not a waste. Rather, I took the decision just to protect myself. She said "oh then you are not a strong Christian," I said no, no, that's not true I was just being careful". We eventually laughed over the matter. When she got back to London, she sent a text message to me, thanking me for hosting her. She remarked in her text "I now know that you are a true Christian". That was how God helped me escape the plan of the enemy to attack my salvation and pull me back into the life of sin.

Dear reader, you and I need to be serious with

the salvation of our souls. Are you saved already? Then you must jealously guard the salvation of your soul with all the wisdom and power that God has given you. In our discourse in the preceding chapters, we have broached some critical issues that prompted God to design a rescue plan, a program of salvation for mankind after the fall of Adam and Eve in the Garden of Eden. Following the violation of God's divine law by our First Parents, the attendant repercussions of their actions were both physical and spiritual death. But God never left us alone in our state of depravity. He designed a rescue plan for us. Indeed, in Genesis 3:15, God made this promise:

And I will put enmity between thee and
the woman, and between thy seed and
her seed; it shall bruise thy head, and thou
shalt bruise his heel.

God's plan of eternal deliverance for man is great salvation which is given freely to all who believe His promise by virtue of our faith in the birth, death, and resurrection of Jesus Christ who was made the propitiation for our sins. Jesus Christ is God's appointed Representative and Substitute for all human beings who believe in the Saviour of the world. Yes, Jesus Christ is the propitiation for the sins of all who believe God and accept His Son, Jesus Christ, as their personal Lord and Saviour. Those who believe will in turn receive salvation. While it is incontrovertible that God is the originator and the driver of the plan of salvation for mankind, it still goes without saying that there are some critical roles that we human beings MUST play so that God's rescue plan for our souls from the fiendish grip of Satan, our arch-enemy, can succeed. As mere mortals, we may find it difficult to have a total comprehension of the need for and the nature of salvation. Nevertheless, it suffices for us to know that salvation is an issue of life and death and hence we must take the issue of the salvation of our souls very seriously.

You Are Not Saved By Your Work

Therefore, my dear friends, as you have
always obeyed—not only in my presence,
but now much more in my absence—
continue to work out your salvation with
fear and trembling, for it is God who works in you to will and to act according to
his good purpose.(Philippians 2:12-13)

In the above scripture, Apostle Paul spoke to a congregation of the early Christians in Philippi and challenged them to work out their salvation with fear and trembling. Now it must be noticed that Paul did not say "work for" your salvation but rather, he asked them to "work out" your salvation.

Working Out Your Salvation, NOT Working For Your Salvation

In his letter to Christians in the City of Ephesus, Apostle Paul emphasized the fact that the salvation of our soul is not a consequence of our work or what we do. It is not about our efforts to be righteous. Simply put, our salvation is not a consequence of our work of righteousness. Not at all. Indeed, The Bible tells us that we were saved by **GRACE THROUGH FAITH** in Jesus Christ Hear Paul speak again:

> **"For it is by grace you have been saved, through faith—and this not from**
> **yourselves, it is the gift of God—not by works, so that no one can boast."**
> Ephesians 2:8-9

Dear reader, I want to believe that by now you should be ready to accept Jesus Christ as your personal Lord and Saviour. You should be thinking seriously about accepting the finished work on the cross of Calvary. When you eventually you do that, the Lord will accept you as His own. You will become one of His children who have been redeemed by the precious blood of the Lamb of God who has taken away your sins.

However, make no mistake about it your salvation is not due to your work of righteousness. According to Apostle Paul, it is God's mercy and grace that you have received. In fact, Apostle Paul even told us in the scriptures that your faith in Jesus Christ, which spurred you to accept Him as your Lord and Saviour, is a gift from God, and therefore, there is no room for you or any other person to indulge in self-glorification or boasting. Salvation is a work done by God.

However, salvation is not simply a work that happens when we are born again. It is a full-time work that continues until we are made or re-molded into the full image of Christ. The work of working-out-our-salvation will end only at death or at the rapture, whichever of them that happens first.In the book of Romans, Apostle Paul brilliantly explained the process that the salvation of a person goes through:

For those God foreknew he also predestined
to be conformed to the likeness of his Son, that
he might be the firstborn among many brothers.
And those he predestined, he also called; those he
called, he also justified; those he justified, he also glorified. Romans 8:29-30

Now, dear reader, for you to understand what Apostle Paul is saying in the above-quoted scriptures, you need to contextualize it, I mean you need to plug yourself into the center of the Pauline thesis. According to Apostle Paul, the salvation of your soul will go through the following process:

1. You were **foreknew** by God as one of the souls that will be saved from going to Hell-Fire.
2. You were **predestined** by God to be saved

3. You were **called** by God to hear the gospel through preachers(just as you are being preached to in this book) and upon hearing, you need to respond in faith to what you have heard (elsewhere) about salvation or what you have read in this book. And the concrete action you should take is to give your life to Jesus Christ.

4. When you give your life to Jesus Christ (which I am earnestly urging you to do), you will become an elect of God whom the **Holy Spirit** would help to conform to the image of Jesus Christ

5. After going through this process of salvation, God Himself will eventually justify you, based on your faith in His Son Jesus Christ and for accepting the finished work on the cross. He will declare you righteous and will glorify you.

6. It is important that you must know that when the process of your salvation is completed, you and all other believers whose salvation is completed in Jesus Christ, willone day fully resemble Jesus Christ.

In the light of the foregoing, we can safely say that God knew before time those that would be saved. He knew those that will, by His grace, be brought into His plan of grace and salvation for mankind, and you, dear reader, you are part of God's plan. He chose you by His mercy and grace to be saved not based on any merit you possess. It was an expression of unmerited favor from your creator to you.

Working Out Your Salvation Day By Day

There is no denying the fact that we were saved by God's grace. Our salvation is not due to our work. Nonetheless, it is dangerous for us to just rely on God's grace and be negligent in striving to be holy in all our thoughts, utterances, and actions. This is what God helped me to do in my experience which I narrated above. We have the duty, on a daily basis, to run away from every appearance of sin which can compromise our salvation. In his advice to Timothy, Apostle Paul counseled him to train himself in holiness. Listen to Paul:

But refuse profane and old wives'
fables, and
exercise thyself rather unto
godliness. For bodily
exercise profiteth little: but
godliness is profitable
unto all things, having promise of
the life that now is,
and of that which is to come. This
is a faithful
saying and worthy of all
acceptation.(1 Tim 4:7)

The emphasis here is playing your part in working out your salvation every day even as you rely on the instructions, guidance, and help of the Holy Spirit. Working out your salvation every day simply means with the help of God, undergoing the process of becoming sanctified. Getting sanctified ---- which is the end-product of working out your salvation---- entails working alongside God.God has His own part to play while you too have your own part to play. God cannot play your part for you because He will not force you (as a free moral agent) to do anything. Nevertheless, it is God that works in us or put it simply, it is God that helps you to work out your salvation by helping you to live a holy life. Hear Paul again:

> **Wherefore, my beloved, as ye havealways**
> **obeyed, not as in my presenceonly, but**
> **now much more in my absence, work out**
> **your own salvation with fear and trembling.**
> **For it is God which worketh in you both to**
> **will and to do of his good pleasure.**
> **Do all things**
> **without murmurings and disputings: That ye**
> **maybe blameless and harmless, the sons of**
> **God, without rebuke, in the midst of a crooked**

**and perverse nation, among whom
ye shine as
lights in the world;**(<u>Philippians
2:12-13</u>)

The Unique Partnership Involved In Working Out Our Salvation

The ordinary meaning of the word partnership is the involvement of more than one person in a business or a project. Yes, just as we do have a partnership in business, the same way we do have a partnership in the spiritual business or spiritual project called salvation. This partnership is spiritual, not temporal. And the people involved in this partnership are:

1. God Himself
2. You, yes you that have been saved by the blood of Jesus Christ.

In this unique partnership, God is the senior partner who is working 24 hours every day while you and I are the junior partners. God is busy working along with you to ensure that His investment in your life yields the desired result. He invested the Blood and the life of His precious Son, Jesus Christ, in your salvation. As Apostle Paul said, God invested His grace upon our lives for us to be saved. Listen to what Paul said about God's investment of His grace on Paul's life:

> **For I am the least of the apostles and do not**
> **even deserve to be called an apostle, because**
> **I persecuted the church of God. But by the**
> **grace of God I am what I am, and his grace to**
> **me was not without effect. No, I worked harder**
> **than all of them—yet not I, but the grace of**
> **God that was with me.** (1 Corinthians 15:9-10)

Paul said he worked harder than everybody else. He also acknowledged the fact that it was not him that was doing the work but the grace of God that was invested in his salvation by God. At the end of the day, Apostle Paul happily declared that God's grace upon his life was not without effect in him.

My dear reader, the truth of this matter is that God's grace works in everyone that accepts Jesus Christ as his or her personal Lord and Saviour. God's grace works in you and me, helping us to grow spiritually. Unfortunately, the works of God's grace have no good results in many people, unlike the case of Paul. The simple reason that makes the work of God's grace to be of no effect in them is that they failed to play their role in the partnership project. They resisted and keep resisting every day the work of the Holy Spirit in their lives.

For the work of God's grace to have an impact in our lives as it did in the life of Apostle Paul, we must work with God in the process of our sanctification. How do we do this? It is by responding to the Holy Spirit's warning and counsel. Whenever He cautions us against sinning or doing bad things, we must listen to Him. We must allowthe Holy

Spirit to empower us to accomplish His will for our lives. We must never make the mistake of boasting about our righteousness because it is God Himself that gives you and I the desire to grow spiritually. He is the One that works in you and me every day, helping us to work out our salvation by living a holy life.

This is why you and I cannot give credit to ourselves for being holy or being righteous because God did it all. Indeed our desire to live a life of holiness; our desire to be righteous or do the right thing all the time; our desire to run away from sin and be holy all these come from God. This is what Apostle Paul meant when he said "God is working in us" God Himself inspires in us the inclination to holiness and desire to make God happy in all our ways.

We Must Learn To Obey God Every Day

> Therefore, my dear friends, as you have
> always obeyed—not only in my presence,

but now much more in my
absence—continue
to work out your salvation with fear
and trembling,
(Philippians 2:12)

Obedience to God's instructions and commandments is an important key to working out our salvation every day. In the above-quoted scripture, Apostle Paul emphasized obedience. Obedience is a very important key in getting sanctified which is the main goal of the efforts we put into working out our salvation every day. After you have given your life to Jesus Christ, the next step you shouldtake is to aim at growing in obedience to God every day. Indeed, you need to be obedient to God to work out your salvation.

Obedience to God is not only a necessary practice in sanctification but it is proof of your salvation. If you claim to be a born again Christian and yet you do not practice daily obedience to God, then your salvation is not genuine. You will

Emmanuel S. Omere

then be among those people the Lord referred to in the Book of Mathew:

> **"Not everyone who says to me,**
> **'Lord, Lord,**
> **'will enter the kingdom of heaven,**
> **but only**
> **he who does the will of my Father**
> **who is**
> **in heaven"** (<u>Matthew 7:21</u>).

Dear reader, while you need to know that obedience to God is not negotiable, it is also imperative for you to know that the *Adamic* nature you were born with has to be discarded before you can obey God. No wonder, Jesus Christ warned that to enter the kingdom of God you and I must be born again, we must get the **new nature** from God. It is this new nature—a nature that desires to practice righteousness—that will help you and me to obey God. Indeed, every born again Christian who is truly part of the kingdom of God will inexorably hunger and thirst for righteousness. Listen to Apostle John:

This is how we know who the children of
God are and who the children of the devil are:
Anyone who does not do what is right is not a
child of God; nor is anyone who does not love
his brother"(1 John 3:10).

When you make it a habit to practice righteousness every day, then it is evident that you are genuinely saved. It means you are determined to always obey God and even when you erred, and you realize it, you will immediately repentand continue to practice obedience to God. Now there is a reward for you for obeying God: you will enjoy His blessings on your lives and you will continue to grow in your sanctification according to Apostle James:

"**But the man who looks intently into the**
perfect law that gives freedom, and

---

continues to do this, not forgetting what he has heard, but doing it—he will be blessed in what he does."James 1:25

The man who obeys God's words will be blessed by God spiritually, he will have good health, wealth, and other things that will come from God such as protection, peace, and other fruits of the Holy Spirit.

Things To Do Daily As You Work Out Your Salvation

1. Engage In Rigorous Study Of The Word Of God.

Before going to the cross, Jesus Christ prayed a very significant prayer for you and I. Hear Him:

"Sanctify them by your truth, your word is truth" (John 17:17).

For us to grow in Christ, we must love the Word of God. We must be devoted to the study, memorization, and meditating in the Word of God. Apostle Peter said:

> **"Like newborn babies, crave pure spiritual**
> **milk, so that by it you may grow up in your**
> **salvation" (1 Peter 2:2).**

The writer of the Book of Hebrew declared thus:

> **For the word of God is quick, and powerful, and**
> **sharper than any two-edged sword, piercing even to**
> **the dividing asunder of soul and spirit, and of the joints**
> **and marrow, and is a discerner of the thoughts and**
> **intents of the heart. Neither is there any creature that**

**is not manifest in his sight: but all
things are naked and
opened unto the eyes of him with
whom we have to do**.
(Heb 4:12-13).

2. Be A Prayer Addict, Engage In Rigorous Prayer.

Again before He went to the cross the Lord told
the disciples:

**"Watch and pray so that you will
not fall
into temptation. The spirit is
willing, but
the body is weak"'**(Mark 14:38).

The import of Jesus' advice is that we must
pray regularly to avoid sin and also to grow
unhindered. We need to be disciplined in prayer
if we are to be obedient to God.

3. Do Not Forsake The Fellowship of Fellow Christians

There is this common saying in the Christendom: Iron sharpeneth iron. Now hear the Word of GodIn<u>Proverbs 27:17</u>:

> **"As iron sharpens iron, so one**
> **Mansharpens another."**

Being around godly brothers and sisters who are serious about Christ will help us to grow.

> **"Therefore confess your sins to**
> **each other**
> **and pray for each other so that**
> **you may**
> **be healed. The prayer of a righteous**
> **man is**
> **powerful and effective"** (<u>James</u>
> <u>5:16</u>).

Who do you seek counsel from and who do you regularly fellowship with? Many Christians have fellowship but their fellowship is centered around things and people God will not approve.

Let our Christian fellowship be centered around spiritual growth and knowing God more.

4. Get Yourself Involved In the Kingdom's Business

If we must grow in Christ, if we must succeed in working out our salvation daily, we must be physically involved in the work of God in our local churches. In his letter to Philemon, Apostle Paul has this to say on this issue:

> **I pray that you may be active in sharing**
> **your faith, so that you will have a full**
> **understanding of every good thing we**
> **have in Christ" (Philemon 1:6**).

Paul told Philemon to be active in sharing his faith because through sharing his faith; by engaging in witnessing, evangelism, and other works in the church, Philemon, and indeed every other believer, will experience spiritual growth and

198

perfection of our salvation. We will, in the words of Paul, come to a full understanding of every good thing believers have in Christ.

Those who have been saved must arise for the salvation of others. We can only do this by serving God in our local churches as the Holy Spirit leads us. If we fail to serve, we are at the risk of going backward andnothaving a full understanding of Christ.

CHAPTER NINE

The Spiritual Imperatives Of Salvation

From the title of this chapter, the key operative word is IMPERATIVES. This is a pointer to the fact that our focus in this chapter will be on certainissues or things that we can consider to be imperatives as far as the issue of salvation is concerned. To begin with, we need to understand the meaning of the word imperative generally and within the context of our discourse on God's plan of salvation for humanity.

The *collinsdictionary.com* described the word imperative as "something that is extremely important and (which) must be done."And to further amplify the meaning of this word—imperatives— we can describe it as thingsor actions that ought to be taken and must be or a decision that should be made, or"something <u>extremely</u> <u>urgent</u> or <u>important</u>, very <u>essential</u>".

All the foregoing are the explanations of the meaning of the word imperative. From our discussions on the issue of salvation thus far, can we really say that some things, situations, or conditionscan be regarded as imperatives of salvation? Are there actions and decisions which are "<u>extremely</u> <u>urgent</u> or <u>important</u>, very <u>essential</u>"and which cannot be deferred when it comes to the issue of salvation?

The Imperatives Of The Cross

Right from the word go, Jesus Christ never left anyone in doubt as to the necessity of His death on the cross and the severe beatings, excruciating pains, sufferings humiliation, and the nailing to the cross which preceded His eventual death. On His way to Jerusalem Jesus Christ reminded His disciples about His MISSION on earth:

And Jesus going up to Jerusalem took the twelve disciples apart in the way, and said unto them, Behold, we go up to Jerusalem; and the Son of man shall be betrayed unto the chief priests and unto the scribes, and they shall condemn him to death, And shall deliver him to the Gentiles to mock, and to scourge, and to crucify him: and the third day he shall rise again. Mathew 20:17-19

Even while in the Garden of Gethsemane, when the import of the agonizing torture, sufferings, beatings, humiliation and death dawn on Him and He asked God the Father to take away the CUP from Him, the Heavenly Father made it known to the Saviour that it was a DIVINE IMPERATIVE that Jesus Christ should die. The Lord accepted it and He did the needful. Hear Him:

> **Then saith he unto them, My soul is exceeding**
> **sorrowful, even unto death: tarry ye here, and watch**
> **with me. And he went a little further, and fell on**
> **his face, and prayed, saying, O my Father, if it be**
> **possible, let this cup pass from me: nevertheless**
> **notas I will, but as thou wilt.**
> (Mathew 26: 38-39)

Going to the Cross at Calvary was not an optional issue for Jesus Christ. It was imperative. Christ emphasized this when He used the word MUST in Mathew 16:21.

> **From that time forth began Jesus to shew unto**
> **his disciples, how that he must go unto Jerusalem,**

and suffer many things of the elders and chief
priests and scribes, and be killed, and be raised
again the third day. Then Peter took him, and
began to rebuke him, saying, Be it far from thee,
Lord: this shall not be unto thee. But he turned, and
said unto Peter, Get thee behind me, Satan: thou art
an offence unto me: for thou savourest not the
things that be of God, but those that be of men.
Matthew 16:21-24

In the Book of Mark, again Christ stressed the imperative of His arrest, torture, and death on the cross:

And they laid their hands on him, and took him.

Andone of them that stood by drew a sword, and smote a servant of the high priest, and cut off his ear. And Jesus answered and said unto them, Are ye come out, as against a thief, with swords and with staves to take me? I was daily with you in the temple teaching, and ye took me not: but the scriptures must be fulfilled
(Mark 14:46-49).

In the Book of John chapter 3 verse 14, Jesus Christ declared:

And as Moses lifted up the serpent in the wilderness, even so must the Son of man be lifted up: That whosoever believeth in him should not perish, but have eternal life.

The MUST Imperative In The Salvation Of Your Soul

Dear reader, in the foregoing, you would have taken note of a certain word which Jesus Christ repeatedly used while stating the imperatives of His death

for Him to accomplish His mission on earth. That word is MUST. Hear the Lord speak again in the book of John and take note of the word MUST:

> **And as Moses lifted up the serpent in the**
> **wilderness, even so MUST the Son of Man**
> **be lifted up, John 3:14.**

In Chapter Nine, the imperative word MUST was also used:

> **I must work the works of Him who sent Me while**
> **it is day; the night is coming when no one can**
> **work.** (John 9:4.)

Just as the issue of Christ's death on the Cross was imperative for Him, you and I must also see the following as our imperatives. They are issues that are of utmost concern to us. They are things that are extremely important and (which) must be done:

a. Believe that Jesus Christ is the ONLY begotten Son of God

b. Believe that He suffered and died for your sins on the cross

c. Believe that He shed His blood on the cross to redeem you and for the remission of your sins

d. Believe that Jesus Christ by His death reconciled you with God the Father and you can now develop a sustainable relationship you're your creator

e. Believe that He paid the price for your sins and thereby saved you from the **SECOND DEATH**which will surely occur to those who did not accept Jesus Christ after they must have physically died on earth.

Salvation Is Personal

An interesting question that should agitate the mind of every reader of this book is "What must I do to be saved?" Or put it in another way, the question can be: What should I do that I have not done?" Here we are talking about very crucial issues. Issues that pertain to yoursouland its home in ETERNITY. Hence the following questions are very germane:

1. **What is the thing that I should do?**
2. **What is the action that I should I take?**
3. **In what direction should I go?**

Indeed, the issue of salvation is a personal one. There is no salvation by a surrogate. And the simple answer to all the above questions is to **believe in the Lord Jesus Christ and you will be saved**. It is important for every living human being on planetearth to know that the issue of our salvation is one that we cannot escape.

The crucial question of what **must I doto be saved** willalways crop up. There is no alternative to the salvation of your soul through Christ Jesus.

Once you can take that decision then you are accepted into the universal family of God and you have become a joint-heir with the Son—Jesus Christ.

Repentance: An Imperative In Salvation

We need to know that as much as we desire to be saved from our sins and enjoy the free offer of salvation which comes via Jesus Christ's death on the cross, there are certain things which we must do before we can be reconciled to our creator and once again become His sons and daughters. One of these things is REPENTANCE FROM SIN.

Whether we like it or not, salvation from your sin is impossible without **repentance**. Indeed, there has to be repentance before there can be salvation.You MUST come to the knowledge of your status as a sinner who has been separated from God firstly by sins of Adam and Eve and secondly by your sins.

And like king David in Psalm 51, dear reader,

we must acknowledge the fact that we have allsinned:

> **For I acknowledge my transgressions: and**
> **my sin is ever before me. Against thee, thee only,**
> **have I sinned,and done this evil in thy sight:**
> **that thou mightest be justified when thou speakest,**
> **and be clear when thou judgest. Behold, I was**
> **shapen in iniquity;and in sin did my mother**
> **conceive me.**[Psa. 51:3]

When we come to see ourselves as sinners, just as David saw himself as a sinner who needed salvation, then the finished work on the cross can be meaningful to us. Thereafter, we can then accept the finished work on the cross. David declared his helplessness:

⁵ Behold, I was shapened in iniquity; and in
sin did my mother conceive me.
Psalm 51:5 King James Version (KJV)

This is very true of every human being that came to this world via Adam and Eve. The very nature we inherited from Adam is corrupt and evil. Our nature is capable and indeed susceptible to sin.

Just as David was, we too must be convinced and be convicted of our sins. The first thing (or if you like, the first imperative) a person desiring salvation must do is to be convicted of his or her sin by the Holy Spirit. We need to examine our lives and accept the fact that God is not happy with our sinful state and that if we do not REPENT, we are heading to HELL

FIRE. That is why it is easy for our sinful nature, our flesh to do all its evil works as Apostle Paul declared in Galatians 5:19-21 :

19 Now the works of the flesh are manifest, which
are these; Adultery, fornication, uncleanness,

lasciviousness, 20 Idolatry, witchcraft, hatred, variance, emulations, wrath, strife, seditions, heresies, 21 Envyings, murders, drunkenness, revellings, and such like: of the which I tell you before, as I have also told you in time past, that they which do such things shall not inherit the kingdom of God.Galatians 5:19-21 King James Version (KJV)

Having repented from our sin and received salvation, we must move on to the state of vigilance and careful living. Daily, we must work out our salvation, being watchful and staying clear of situations and things that can enslave us to sin again. Also on a daily basis, we will be experiencing the "joy of salvation" just like David. Unfortunately today, a lot of believers cannot experience this joy because of sinsthat they have refused to confess.

It is imperative for every believer who has

experienced the new birth to have the desire to live for God by living a holy and righteous life. If we indeed believe Jesus Christ died ahorrible death on the cross andbore in His body our sins, then we must live for the honor and glory of God.

CHAPTER TEN

Are You Ready For His Second Coming?

M any years ago, Satan launched a serious attack to make me turn back from THE WAY. He knew that when I was in his fold, had a serious weakness when it comes to women. Bur, glory be to the merciful God who delivered me from the trap of the enemy and broke and destroyed the power of adultery and sexual immorality in my life. The bait Satan used was a lady I dated while I wasn't a born-again Christian. I dated the lady for five years before I quitted the relationship. Something happened that made me to severe the relationship with her. I went as far as deleting her numbers from my phone. And what is more, when I became born-again I completely steered clear of her. I didn't talk to her again or have anything to do with her.

But one day I went to the supermarket and I ran into this lady. She was surprised to see me and she was excited to see me.

"Why have you stayed away from me",

she asked with a tinge of excitement in her voice

"Oh, I just decided to go to Christ. If you are not in

Christ, then you are in crises", I exclaimed.

I told her further that the life I was living before I met Christ was not good; that wasn't the type of life God wanted me to live so I had to change. I asked her too if she had met Christ and she answered in the affirmative. She said she has joined The Latter Day Saints Church, The Church of Mormon. She appeared to want us to revive our relationship because she said she had missed the fun we used to have together.

Indeed, before I cut off the relationship, almost every weekend, we used to visit one restaurant or the other. It was a new restaurant per weekend.

People thought we were husband and wife. So, she quickly wrote her mother's phone number on a piece of paper and asked me to call her as she was entering her car. And we parted ways.

As I was walking back to my car, the Holy Spirit ministered to me that I was on my way back to the world again. It dawned on me that there was no way this lady will come to my house and something will not happen between us. I then brought out the piece of paper containing her phone number and tore it into pieces and put it in the trash. I then went back home. I had to take the issue of the salvation of my soul seriously. How I wish every churchgoer will take the issue of the salvation of their soul seriously! Indeed, we must know that the issue of the salvation of our souls is of paramount importance to God. The matter of salvation is not a trivial thing at all because it has to do with what happens to you after you depart from this present world. That is why you must take it seriously. The Bible told us in the Book of Hebrew Chapter 9 verse 27, how important it is for a man or a woman to ensure that he or she is saved by the Blood of the Lamb of God--- Jesus Christ. Listen to the Scriptures:

> **And as it is appointed unto men once to**
> **die, but after this the judgment:**
> **Hebrews 9:27 King James Version (KJV)**

So, the matter of salvation is a matter of life and death. It is about where you will spend your eternity whether in heaven with Jesus Christ or in Hell-fire with Satan and his demons. It is therefore not surprising that God never spared any effort in instituting an infallible redemption plan for the salvation of mankind from sin for us all to be saved and inherit a blissful eternity with Him in heaven.

Jesus Christ The pivot

The pivot of God's divine plan for man's salvation is Jesus Christ. Central to God's plan is the inevitable death of God's only begotten Son, Jesus Christ on the cross. Without His death and the shedding of His Blood, there can be no remission of sin. Indeed, the death of Jesus Christ brought salvation to all men and women, boys, and girls who accept Him as their Lord and Personal Saviour. Yes, everyone, young or old, who believe Jesus Christ and allow Him to rule their lives are saved.

Today, across all the continents in the world, we have billions of people who have confessed Jesus Christ as their Lord and Saviour, they claimed to be saved, but the evidence of genuine salvation is lacking in their lives. These people believe they're saved, but they are not saved! On the other hand, we have people who indeed are truly are saved but are still uncomfortable; they are struggling with the assurance of their salvation. But before we go further, let's take a look at the issue of what can be considered to be evidence of genuine salvation which must be empirically seen and verifiable in the life of a person who claimed to be saved. Related to this is the issue of assurance of salvation.

1. Unwavering Faith, Hope, And Trust in God

Every genuinely saved person is expected to have unwavering faith in the Lord. He or she is supposed to put his or her absolute trust in Jesus Christ who is his or her Saviour. Dear reader, if indeed you are genuinely saved, this evidence should manifest in your life. Your trust in the Lord must not waver irrespective of the daily challenges of life. Now, listen to the Lord Jesus as He speaks on this matter:

> **"And Jesus answering, said to them, Verily I say to you, if you have faith, without wavering, you may do not only as much as is done to this fig tree; but if you should even say to that mountain, Be thou lifted up and thrown into the sea, it shall be done (Matthew 21:21)**

When you are truly saved, there will be no confusion or doubt in your mind. Your trust or faith in Him will be solid, unwavering! Your confidence and reliance on Him will be irreproachable. Come what may, you will be steady at all times. Your steadfast faith and hope in God will be firm at all times. Such faith and hope cannot be weakened by the vicissitudes of life. Now, listen to King Solomon in this scripture:

> **Trust in the Lord with all thine heart;**
> **and lean not unto thine own understanding.**
> **6 In all thy ways acknowledge him, and he**
> **shall direct thy paths. (Proverb 3:5 KJV)**

As a genuinely saved person, you must not allow disappointments of life to change your focus on the Lord Jesus Christ. As a child of God, whether you have just given your life to Jesus Christ or you have been born again for a long while, it is sure that you will face some disappointments of life which may tempt you to depend upon yourself. But rather than leaning unto your understanding, you should live the life God has planned for you as His favorite child and rest in God's understanding because He possesses all wisdom according to Apostle Paul.

> **"Oh, the depth of the riches of the wisdom**
> **and knowledge of God! How unsearchable**
> **his judgments, and his paths beyond**
> **tracing out!"**
> (Romans 11:33)

Indeed, trusting in the Lord sometimes does come with some prices to be paid. It may bring about some great difficulties. Yet, we must not waver. We must be undeterred. Every day of our lives we must allow God to have His way. We must "acknowledge him, and he shall direct our paths". When you have done this, you can then approach the Throne of Grace and cry out to

Heaven, like the Psalmist, and say vindicate me O LORD:

> **Vindicate me, O Lord, for I have walked in my**
> **integrity; And I have trusted in the Lord without**
> **wavering. 2 Examine me, O Lord, and try me;**
> **Test my mind and my heart. 3 For Thy loving kindness is before my eyes, And**
> **I have walked in Thy truth. 4 I do not sit with**
> **deceitful men, Nor will I go with pretenders.**
> Judge me, O LORD, for I have walked in mine
> integrity, and I have trusted in the LORD
> without wavering.Psalms 26:1

Dear reader when you find yourself in difficult situations in life, which is inevitable, you must not think that God does not care about you as many people do. Never you query God and ask foolish questions like:

"Why do bad things happen to me even after I have given my life to Jesus?"

Do not say:

"God, where are you? You are not showing up when I need you".

Indeed, we as children of God who have been genuinely saved by the precious blood of His son, Jesus Christ, will always be, and ever remain the apple of God's eyes. He will never forsake us. Even amid the turmoil of life, God will continue to stick with His children and use challenges of life to shape their lives. My dear reader of this book, you must understand this important fact. When you can understand this fact of life, any challenge or setback that may come your way will be seen as instruments that God is using to work on your life.

My beloved reader God cares for you and me and all His children all over the world, those who are genuinely saved wherever they are in the world. Here are the comforting words of the Lord:

> **"And surely I am with you always,**
> **to the**
> **very end of the age."**
> (<u>Matthew 28:20b</u>)

2. Conviction Of Sin And Hatred For Sin

To be convinced of sin that you have committed and also realize the fact that you need to steer clear of sin, is another evidence that your salvation is genuine. To begin with, we must know that sin is rooted in our old nature which we inherited from Adam and Eve. Except a person becomes born again and he or she is regenerated by the Holy Spirit, he or she will remain in that state of a natural man or a natural woman which was transferred to every progeny of Adam and Eve.

A natural person will continue to grow and develop every day with his or her sinful nature. Only an encounter with the Saviour—Jesus

Christ—can change the situation. Indeed, every thought conceived by a natural man or a natural woman, every word spoken by him or her as well as every action is taken by him or her will be driven by this sinful nature. This is the awful state in which a person who has not been saved exists. And alas! Such a person will see nothing wrong in his state. Nothing has gone amiss. And this is because he or she has not had an encounter with the Lord Jesus Christ. However, in the words of Apostle Paul, such a person is in a state of spiritual death because he or she is carnally minded and not spiritually-minded. The spiritual death, anyway, came about as a result of Adam's and Eve's sin. Let's hear Apostle Paul talk through the leading of the Holy Spirit:

> For to be carnally minded is death;
> but to be
> spiritually minded is life and peace.
> Because the
> carnal mind is enmity against God:
> for it is not

subject to the law of God, neither indeed can be.

Romans 8:6-7 King James Version (KJV)

Thus, it takes a person who has been genuinely saved to take note and understand the dangerous import of the natural nature that all human beings inherited from Adam and Eve. Genuine salvation, which God gives through His Son Jesus Christ, is the only antidote to our sinful nature. When genuine salvation comes, we will understand the proclivity of man's nature as far as sin is concerned. We will also know why it is difficult for man to steer clear of sin.It is only a genuinely saved person that can abhor sin. He or she is the one who will pray every day for power to overcome sin and also crave salvation from sin and deliverance from the sinful nature of man which is the source of sin.

Dear reader, I want you to know that if you can give your life to Jesus Christ, the Lord will send the Holy Spirit to you and the Holy Spirit will work on your sinful nature. The Lord will quicken your mortal mind, then you will constantly desire that nature that hates sin. Only God can give you this nature when you become genuinely saved.

Indeed, it takes a person that is genuinely saved to know that sin is evil. Such a person will be convicted of his sin by the Holy Spirit whenever he or she erred. Such genuine conviction of sin should drive the person to Jesus Christ. The conviction of sin will lead the person to realize the fact that he or she needs a Saviour---Jesus Christ. And when the consequence of sin dawns on him or her, He or she will become alarmed and distressed. Being convinced of his or her guilt, he or she will long for a pardon because he or she knows the dire consequences of his or her sin and he is concerned for his safety. He will then cry out: " O God be merciful to me, a wretched sinner!" He or she will come unto the Lord to receive forgiveness for his or her sins after confessing them.

3. Perfect Hatred For Sin

Here is another evidence of genuine salvation. Every genuinely saved person must manifest a holy hatred for sin. Sin is abhorrent, it is evil because it is the opposite of what our Holy God likes or wants. Sin is disrespectful to the instructions, order, directives, and commandments of God. It is an insult to our God. Sin, therefore, is the transgression of God's law:

> **4 Whosoever committeth sin transgresseth also**
> **the law: for sin is the transgression of the law.**
> **1 John 3:4 King James Version (KJV)**

The simple reason why God hates sin is that it is antithetical to God's nature. Sin is the work of the devil as our Lord Jesus declared in the scripture:

> **44 Ye are of your father the devil, and the lusts of**
> **your father ye will do. He was a murderer from the**
> **beginning, and abode not in the truth, because there**

**is no truth in him. When he
speaketh a lie, he
speaketh of his own: for he is a
liar, and the
father of it. (John 8:44 KJV)**

As we have noted in previous chapters, sin disrupted Adam's and Eve's fellowship with God. Sin is a perversion of the good things that God created. Hence, dear reader, it is imperative for you to hate sin because the consequences of sin are the unbearable wrath of God. Sin brings dire consequences. Sin is deceitful and brings about physical and spiritual death.

**14 But every man is tempted, when
he is drawn
away of his own lust, and enticed.
15 Then when
lust hath conceived, it bringeth
forth sin: and sin,
when it is finished, bringeth forth
death.
(James 1:14-15 KJV)**

Oftentimes, the consequences of sin are painful. Indeed, the outcomes of sin are abhorrent and hideous. But unfortunately, while we hate the consequences of sin, we don't as much hate sin, the agent which produces these hurtful outcomes. Don't get me wrong, my dear reader, yes, we should hate how sin hurts us because the consequences of sin are calamitous--- separation from God, sickness, poverty, shame, regret, guilt, and fear just to mention a few. But we must also do everything to attack the root of all these pains which is SIN. Above all, sin is a hindrance to a godly and holy life. It sentences a person to eternal damnation and separation from God.

> **2 But your iniquities have separated between you and your God, and your sins have hid his face from you, that he will not hear. For your hands are defiled with blood, and your fingers with iniquity; your lips have spoken lies, your tongue hath muttered perverseness. (Isaiah 59:2-3 KJV)**

This is dreadful! All these are detestable products of sin. Shouldn't we now give due attention to SIN which is the cause or the source of these hurtful outcomes? Indeed, there is no need for hesitation any longer, we must run away from sin because it is awful. When you are tempted to sin, remember that there is a serious penalty for your action. And come to think of it, why must you suffer again after Someone has suffered for you and died on your behalf? Yes, Jesus Christ bled and died because of your sin

4. An Inexorable Appetite For Divine Things

> **6 Blessed are they which do hunger and thirst after righteousness: for they shall be filled.**
> **(Matthew 5:6-7 KJV)**

A strong aversion for mundane things and passion for divine things is another evidence that someone is genuinely saved. In his letter to

Christians in Rome, Apostle Paul warned us about carnality. He posited that everyone that has had an encounter with Jesus Christ (i.e. a person who has surrendered his or her life to Jesus Christ as I am urging you to do my dear reader), must be spiritually minded. He or she should no longer be ruled or controlled by the sinful nature which we inherited from Adam and Eve. Anyone living in a contrary way is carnally minded and to be carnally minded is death.

Now, when a person's strong appetite, satisfaction, pleasure, and delight are centered on things of this world, such a person is carnally minded. He or she will be spiritually dead. He or she will have little or no interest for Divine or spiritual things. Such a person is dead in sin; dead while he or she is still alive. On the contrary, when you, my dear reader, decide to have a burning desire, unquenchable thirst for God, know very well that you are spiritually minded and that you are alive in the spirit.

Again, when you have a strong desire to be in the presence of God and you enjoy the fellowship of Christian brethren, then you are spiritually-minded. When you feel God's love, when you always receive His blessings and walk in the light of His countenance, then you are spiritually-minded. These desire of yours for divine things are clear evidence of the genuineness of your salvation

> **6 Blessed are they which do hunger and thirst**
> **after righteousness: for they shall be filled.**
> **Matthew 5:6-7 King James Version (KJV)**

My beloved reader of this book, I want to urge you to always have the desire to please Jesus Christ. Always make it a point of duty to make Him happy in all your ways at all times. Always pray for the grace to make Jesus Christ the focus of your daily pursuit and desires. If you do this, then, you are the redeemed of the Lord. You cannot die spiritually and you will always have a strong appetite for spiritual things.

Printed in the United States
by Baker & Taylor Publisher Services

Printed in the United States
by Baker & Taylor Publisher Services